IDEA WISE Bathrooms

Inspiratio
for the Do

Jerri Farris

Creative Publishing international

CHANHASSEN, MINNESOTA
www.creativepub.com

Creative Publishing
international

Copyright © 2005
Creative Publishing international, Inc.
18705 Lake Drive East
Chanhassen, Minnesota 55317
1-800-328-3895
www.creativepub.com

Printed in China

10 9 8 7 6 5 4 3 2 1

President/CEO: Ken Fund
Vice President/Publisher: Linda Ball
Vice President/Retail Sales & Marketing: Kevin Haas

Executive Editor: Bryan Trandem
Creative Director: Tim Himsel
Managing Editor: Tracy Stanley

Author: Jerri Farris
Editor: Thomas Lemmer
Book Designer: Kari Johnston
Technical Illustrator: Rich Stromwall
Photo Researcher: Julie Caruso
Production Manager: Helga Thielen

IdeaWise: Bathrooms

Library of Congress
Cataloging-in-Publication Data

Farris, Jerri.
 Ideawise bathrooms : inspiration & information for the
do-it-yourselfer / by Jerri Farris.
    p. cm.
 ISBN 1-58923-203-8 (soft cover)
 1. Bathrooms--Remodeling--Amateurs' manuals. 2. Bathrooms--
Design and construction--Amateurs' manuals. 3. Do-it-yourself
work. I. Title.
 TH4816.3.B37F37 2005
 643'.52--dc22
                                                    2005007704

Table of Contents

Introduction

Folk wisdom tells us that everything old is new again, an idea that is as true of bathrooms as anything else. Today's trend watchers report that the average family bath has doubled in size since the 1950s and that large, comfortable bathrooms including luxurious baths and showers are second only to gourmet kitchens on the list of upscale home buyers' requests.

This information is reported as news in industry magazines, regarded as a burgeoning trend, and catered to by manufacturers, building contractors, and designers. All the while, we collectively imagine that we are—at this moment in history—somehow unique in our interest in bathrooms.

And yet, in the Minoan Palace of Knossos on the isle of Crete, archeologists found what many believe was the first flushing "water closet," or toilet, circa 1700 B.C. Tiled bathrooms and self-draining tubs connected to underground piping have been discovered in the ruins of Olynthus, a city destroyed by Philip of Macedon in 432 B.C.

There's no doubt that elaborate baths and showers are popular today, but no more so than in ancient Rome, where public baths were the centers of entertainment and gossip. After all, the baths of Diocletian are said to have seated over 3,000 bathers.

Such marvels of plumbing were destroyed along with the ancient civilizations that built and enjoyed them. It took over 3,000 years for another flushing toilet to be devised by J. D. Harrington in 1596, and several hundred more years for modern plumbing to find its way to the general population.

Modern plumbing literally changed the world, reducing as it did the spread of typhus, cholera, and other bacteria-borne disease. A new, expanded, or redecorated bathroom probably won't change your world, but it certainly can radically improve your everyday experience of it. After all, an attractive, functional bathroom soothes, rejuvenates, revives, refreshes, and comforts us.

As the world outside our doors fill with stress and distress, we're investing more and more in our homes, trying to turn them into islands of peace and calm and rest.

Improving or adding a bathroom typically is a sound investment. In most regions of the country, about 90 percent of the money invested in a bathroom remodeling project is returned at the sale of the house—more if the project adds a master bathroom or a second bathroom to a one-bathroom home. Local real estate brokers and building contractors can give you more information on what you can expect in your region.

The National Kitchen and Bath Association, an organization of professional kitchen and bath planners, offers worksheets and self-surveys to help you assess your needs and wants, design guidelines, and connections to professionals in your area at their website nkba.com. The NKBA is an excellent source of both information and inspiration—a good place to start.

Accessibility Matters

Adults with no physical challenges of any sort are not the norm, they are the exception by far. In fact, according to some counts less than 25 percent of the adult population can claim such status. And yet, when accessibility is mentioned in regard to bathrooms, most people conjure up images of austere, clinical looking rooms filled with unattractive adaptive devices, utilitarian fixtures and not much style. That may have been true at some point, but it most definitely is not true today.

The issue of accessibility has evolved into concern for Universal Design—design that works for everyone. Universal Design addresses issues from slip-resistant flooring to adequate lighting, from grab bars and curbless showers to counter height—issues of concern for every body, every age, every size. Addressing these issues adds to everyone's enjoyment of a bathroom and it by no means detracts from its design or style. Today's cabinets, fixtures, and fittings are as attractive as they are functional.

As you choose your bathroom fixtures and materials, consider improving the safety and accessibility of your bathroom as part of your project. Many products that enhance safety and accessibility can easily be installed in less than an hour. During a major renovation project, integrating these features is even easier. When considering safety and ease of use, you'll need to include nearly all aspects of the bathroom: flooring, fixtures, cabinets, showers and tubs, electrical systems, and doors.

How to Use This Book

The pages of *IdeaWise Bathrooms* are packed with images of interesting, attractive, efficient bathrooms. And although we hope you enjoy looking at them, they're more than pretty pictures: they're inspiration accompanied by descriptions, facts, and details meant to help you plan your bathroom project wisely.

Some of the rooms you see here will suit your sense of style, while others may not appeal to you at all. If you're serious about remodeling or building a new bathroom, read every page—there's as much to learn in what you don't like as in what you do. Look at each photograph carefully and take notes. The details you gather are the seeds from which areas for your new bathroom will sprout.

IdeaWise Bathrooms contains six chapters, Walls, Floors and Ceilings; Storage and Display; Fixtures; Fittings; Lighting and Ventilation; and Accessories. In each chapter you'll find several features, each of which contains a specific type of information.

*Design*Wise features hints and tips—insider tricks—from professional bathroom planners. Special thanks to DeWitt Talmadge Beall, Pat Currier, Linda Burkhardt, Trudy McCollum, Deborah Foucher Stuke and Jeff Livingston, and Lori Jo Krengel.

*Dollar*Wise describes money-saving ideas that can be adapted to your own plans and circumstances.

*Idea*Wise illustrates a clever do-it-yourself project for each topic.

Some chapters also include *Words to the* Wise, a glossary of terms that may not be familiar to you.

Another important feature of *IdeaWise Bathrooms* is the Resource Guide on pages 136 to 139. The Resource Guide contains as much information as possible about the photographs in the book, including contact information for architects, designers, and manufacturers when available.

CHAPTER 1

Walls, Floors and Ceilings

The walls, floor, and ceiling define a room: its size, shape, appearance, and—most of all—the ways it's used. That's right: the ways it's used. Surface treatments divide bathrooms into wet and dry zones, areas that can and cannot withstand constant exposure to water.

Like beauty, walls, floors, and ceilings are more than just skin deep. For example, although the surface tile virtually defines an area as a wet zone, the underlying wall material itself must stand up to moisture.
No matter what the surface treatment, cementboard should be used in wet zones rather than drywall.

Some bathroom floors have to be built to carry a serious load. Think about it: a gallon of water weighs about 8.34 pounds, and a two-person tub can hold up to 120 gallons of water. That's about 1000 pounds of dead weight, even before you and your sweetie settle in for a long soak. No wonder the floors beneath large tubs and whirlpools require additional structural support.

In this chapter, you'll see walls, floors, and ceilings in many shapes, sizes, and finishes. Take a look at everything. The most obvious choice isn't always the best option.

Mixing surface coverings and colors on the walls, floors, and ceiling creates an interesting, dynamic room. Here, large square tile covers the floor, tub deck, and backsplash; wallpaper covers the upper walls; and the painted ceiling complements the room's color palette.

Painting the horizontal planes of the coffered ceiling emphasizes its details.

Painted to match the ceiling, the vent grille blends subtly into the surface of the ceiling.

Scrubbable wallcovering is water resistant and durable, a characteristic that's especially important in family bathrooms.

Ceramic tile protects the walls in the splash zone and the deck surrounding the tub.

Check the label—floor tile should have a MOHS scale (a one-to-ten scale of hardness) rating of at least 6 or 7 and a friction coefficient of at least .6, the minimum standard for the Americans with Disabilities Act. (Remember: the higher the coefficient rating, the more slip resistant the tile.)

Walls

Never given much thought to the bathroom walls? You're not alone. Other than old jokes about the writing on them, bathroom walls don't get much attention. However, the walls typically present the largest surface in a bathroom and anyone who ignores them misses a wealth of design opportunities.

Words to the Wise

Cementboard: A substrate used under ceramic tile and stone. Cementboard remains stable even when exposed to moisture, a critical issue in bathrooms.

Fiber/cementboard: A thin, high-density underlayment used in wet areas where floor height is a concern.

Greenboard: Drywall treated to withstand occasional moisture. It's a good choice for bathroom walls outside wet zones.

Drywall: Panels consisting of a gypsum core covered in paper.

Painted drywall is a perennial favorite because paint is inexpensive, attractive and oh-so-easy to change. If you use the right type of paint and apply it properly to the right drywall material, the walls will look great for as long you want to live with the color. And—perhaps best of all—a gallon or two of paint and a free afternoon is all it takes to give the room a facelift when color trends or your tastes change.

Be sure walls in wet zones start with cementboard; greenboard is appropriate for walls outside the wet zones. (See *Words to the* Wise.)

Look for specially-formulated paint with an additive that helps prevent the growth of mold and mildew. (Even so, it's vital to provide ventilation. Run a vent fan when bathing or showering and open the windows when possible.)

Trompe l'oile ("fool the eye") painting techniques create fantasy worlds in bathrooms. The acrylic paints typically used for trompe l'oile are durable enough for bathrooms, even heavily used family baths.

Here, the painter presents a koi's-eye view of a water garden. The theme is continued in the stained-glass treatment of the window, the decorative sink, and the mosaic tile countertop. Subtle touches such as these water-colored towels and soap reinforce a dramatic theme without reaching the level of overkill, which is especially important in a small room.

Medicine cabinets can be nestled between wall studs quite easily in non-load-bearing walls. It's possible to do this in load-bearing walls as well, but generally requires that support be added to transfer the load to the surrounding framing.

Wallpaper dresses a wall like nothing else, and—after a decade-long absence—it's returning to the forefront of the decorating scene. With reasonably priced laser levels available everywhere, it's easier than ever to get it straight.

Wallpaper labeled "scrubbable" is made to withstand exposure to moisture, which is especially important in a family or often-used bathroom. Still, humidity has to be controlled in bathrooms that include wallpaper: Install an efficient vent fan and use it while showering or bathing.

Used in bathing rooms for centuries, ceramic tile is still the number one material chosen for today's bathrooms, probably because it's so versatile. Tile can be smooth or rough, intricate or simple, colorful or muted. It provides excellent insulation, resists fading in any light, repels moisture, and doesn't give off toxic fumes in a fire. And it's so easy to clean that tile rated as "impervious" is often used in operating rooms and commercial kitchens, where cleanliness can be a matter of life and death.

Wall tile is thinner than floor tile and sometimes has a finer finish. You can use floor tile on walls but it's thicker and heavier, which can make it difficult to set. Also, fewer styles of trim are available for floor tile, which may make it harder to finish off all the edges.

Wall layouts are sometimes elaborate and tend to have lots of exposed edges, so manufacturers offer a variety of trim and border pieces for wall tile.

Most wall tile is self-spacing, which means the individual tiles have small flanges on each edge to help maintain even spacing.

Sophisticated techniques allow tile manufacturers to produce tile that imitates natural stone,
metal, and other materials, often at lower prices.

*The combination of subtle color and
glazing give this porcelain tile the
look of polished stone.*

Imagination and innovative materials take bathroom walls to extraordinary heights.

These wall panels aren't tile or stone, but concrete. That's right: concrete. Today, concrete is being used in a surprising number of places—anywhere one might put tile, laminate, solid surface, or natural stone.

Wall panels like these—as well as the tub surround—are cast, then hand polished and sealed to make them stain and water resistant. Concrete is a fabulous material, adored by those willing to accept its eccentricities. Devotees consider the variations in color and texture and the characteristic hair-line cracks a part of its appeal.

If you're considering concrete in your bathroom, talk with your designer or supplier first, and make sure you understand the nature of concrete and the care it requires.

Sealer and paste or beeswax help concrete panels repel water and stains. The finish requires maintenance every three months or so.

Here, solid-surface material mimics the look of marble to create a striking accent in this tight corner of the room.

Smooth river rock set in mortar adds texture to this contemporary bath, proving that stone doesn't need to be cut or polished to be attractive. Filled with irregular shapes, the rock wall is balanced by the smooth lines of the rest of the room. Other elements in the room should support rather than compete with dominant features, such as this wall.

(above) White tile and fixtures sparkle against the mellow tones of tongue-and-groove wood in this spa-like bathroom. Wood brings warmth and richness to any room, but careful thought and preparation is required to keep wood beautiful in a bathroom.

Some wood—such as teak, bamboo, and cedar—is naturally water resistant and, with the application of special sealers, can safely be used on walls as well as floors and even countertops.

Long a favorite in bathrooms, painted beadboard walls lend a traditional air to modern bathrooms. Paint seals the wood, protecting it against moisture and stains. Semigloss or gloss paint, sometimes referred to as "enamel," provides the best protection.

Floors

Bathroom floors have a pretty tough assignment: they need to stand up to drips, drops, and splashes of water, remain safe and comfortable in any situation, and look good while performing these remarkable feats.

Let's talk safety first. More than 25 percent of all household accidents happen in the bathroom. Falls while getting in or out of the tub are the most common household accident, a fact that points out how important it is to choose slip-resistant flooring.

If you're considering tile or stone, check the labeling for something called a "Friction Coefficient," which rates slip resistance. Floor tile must have a friction coefficient of at least .6 to meet standards set by the Americans with Disabilities Act, a good guideline to follow. If the floor covering you're considering isn't labeled this way, ask your designer, contractor, or retailer for more information on slip resistance.

Some floor coverings are undeniably appealing but can't tolerate exposure to water. These floor coverings simply don't belong in bathrooms, where water is the name of the game. Unless bathroom flooring is water resistant or well sealed, problems will develop. Talk with your designer, contractor, or retailer to make sure the floor covering and/or finishes you choose are appropriate.

And, finally, we come to appearance. With the range of reasonably priced materials available, there's no reason to settle for anything less than a floor you love. Keep shopping until you find the colors, textures, and designs that fit your taste and lifestyle.

Horizontal lines in the design visually expand small spaces.

Subtle colors in striking combinations produce a dramatic floor for this luxurious bath. Although the stone is set in a fairly simple pattern, the color combination gives it zing. Stone extends up the walls as well, seamlessly integrating the floor and walls to make the room appear larger than it actually is.

Smooth stone, especially marble, can be cold to the touch. If you love the look of stone but hate to step from a warm shower onto an icy floor, consider a radiant heating system. Radiant floor heat consists of a network of wires or water lines running between the subfloor and the floor covering that keeps even stone floors toasty.

Reasonable prices, durability, and ease of maintenance make vinyl an attractive alternative for bathroom floors. Available in a wide range of patterns and textures, manufacturers offer a product to suit any decor.

Here, the look of brick provides a strong foundation for a room that blends traditional and contemporary influences.

(below) Vinyl flooring in a faux- crocodile pattern gives this contemporary bathroom exotic flair.

Light colors and simple lines contrast beautifully with dark, dramatic floors.

The faux-crocodile texture provides excellent slip resistance.

Flooring Options

Each type of flooring has unique characteristics and installation techniques. Appearance is important, but so are safety, durability, ease-of-care, and environmental impact.

VINYL

Inexpensive, easy to clean, and durable, vinyl flooring is available in a huge variety of colors, patterns, and styles.

Sheet vinyl with felt backing is glued to the subfloor.

Sheet vinyl with PVC backing is glued only along the edges, called a perimeter bond.

Vinyl tiles, which typically come in 12 or 16" squares, generally are not the best choice for bathrooms because the seams leave the subfloor vulnerable to water damage.

CERAMIC TILE

Ceramic tile is made from clay pressed into shape and then fired in a kiln. Glazed ceramic or porcelain tile produces superior bathroom floors—durable, water resistant, and colorful. Porous and softer than glazed tile, unglazed tile is rarely an ideal choice for a bathroom. If used, it must be well sealed and carefully maintained.

Ceramic tile is set in thin-set mortar and then grouted. It's a step-by-step process that requires time and careful planning.

NATURAL STONE

Granite, marble, slate, limestone, and travertine are available in slab and tile form. Stone requires careful upkeep when used in bathrooms, particularly marble. The most easily stained of the natural stones, marble has to be sealed with penetrating sealer and maintained regularly.

HARDWOOD

Hardwood floors look and feel warm; they're also durable and easy to clean. Properly sealed and maintained they can be used in bathrooms, but be aware of the upkeep and precautions required before choosing hardwood for a bathroom.

BAMBOO

Bamboo flooring is durable, attractive, and environmentally sound. Bamboo is a sustainable resource because it regenerates in three to five years. Like wood, it can be used in bathrooms if properly prepared and maintained.

LINOLEUM

Linoleum is an all-organic laminate, a layer made from linseed oil, wood flour, and pine resins bonded to a jute backing. It's kind to the environment, allergy sufferers and chemically sensitive people.

CONCRETE

Polished concrete is available with any number of decorative finishes from matte to super glossy—even an acid-etched surface that can look like stone or marble. Depending on the finish, it may require a fair amount of maintenance. Some manufacturers recommend waxing their concrete products monthly and stripping and resealing it quarterly. Shop around for a product and finish that meet your needs. Also, keep in mind that concrete develops hairline cracks, one of its charms for enthusiasts, but a characteristic that may not be loved by everyone.

Another concern with concrete: weight. Any floor may require additional support, and in the upper stories of wood-framed homes, concrete floors simply may not be practical. Check with a contractor or building inspector for support requirements before investing in concrete floors.

Sometimes you want the floor to
be the star of the show; sometimes you
don't. Here, a simple cream square tile floor
lets the tile-clad walls handle the spotlight.

Glazed tile doesn't need to be sealed, but
grout does. After it has fully cured (check manufacturer's directions), apply grout sealer to the
grout lines only. Using a small sponge brush or
special wheel-like applicator makes it much easier to keep the sealer where you want it.

*When you want the floor to recede,
choose grout that blends rather than
contrasts with the tile. Less contrast
helps the tile meld into the room;
more contrast makes it pop.*

*Profiled backsplash tiles match the
floor and tub surround.*

*Three different rectangular tiles create an
intriguing border for this tub surround.*

*Edge tile have to be individually
cut to complete a diagonal set.*

Tile collections create eye-popping
designs. These collections often include different sizes, shapes, and finishes of the same tile—
sometimes even different tones of the same
color. Here, tile in various shapes and finishes
are combined to dramatic effect. Highly polished tiles cover the walls, while matte finished
versions of the same tile make up the floor.

Diagonal sets require some extra cutting for
the edge tile and setting one section of tile on
the diagonal within a straight set requires a second set of reference lines. However, once the
lines are drawn, diagonal sets are no more difficult than straight.

Tile extends from the vanity area to the bathing area in this master suite. A woven pattern is maintained throughout, but blue accents give way to solid color in the next room. The result is a smooth transition from one space to the next.

If you have a large bathroom, there's no rule that the entire floor all needs to be identical. Create visual separation between areas with accents, borders, and other trim.

*Idea*Wise

Want an easy way to create a floor that makes a statement? Go mosaic. It's amazingly easy to create patterns—even elaborate designs—when you start with mosaic tile mounted to mesh backings. Reasonably priced prearranged borders are widely available at home centers and tile stores.

For extra pizzaz lay a prearranged border at the perimeter of the room,

then connect the floors to the walls with a combination of baseboard tile, borders, and liners.

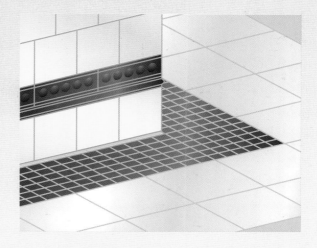

Light washes the walls, illuminating the tile as well as the room.

A spectacular, specially fabricated wood-and-glass sink floats against the wall.

The first floor tile and the top and bottom wall tile are cut to an equal size, which balances the layout.

A wooden mat occupies the floor in front of the sink, providing a slip-resistant surface in this wet zone.

Unique fixtures and accessories glow against the sleek flannel-gray floor and walls of this contemporary bathroom. A solid gray material might have been boring here, but the subtle color variations of this tile keep the background interesting.

Careful planning is vital to this look: Minimizing cut tile and grout lines helps the individual pieces of granite meld into a harmonious whole.

The natural colors of slate set a rich color scheme for this striking, somewhat masculine-looking bathroom. The wall covering, countertop, and even the sink vessel and toilet relate to the deep tones found in the slate.

Choose slate for a bathroom floor only if you understand and appreciate its properties. Because it's a relatively soft material, slate requires periodic maintenance and shows wear over time, especially scratches. Slate is a good choice for those who enjoy materials that reflect the passage of time, but may not be the ideal choice for someone who prefers materials that look new forever.

Cut tiles form baseboards, creating a smooth transition from floor to wall.

*Design*Wise

DeWitt Talmadge Beall

DeWitt Designer Kitchens
Studio City, CA

- Install heating mats under tile or stone to provide a warm and friendly surface for bare feet.

- Create a rug-like pattern in tile or stone by setting tile on the diagonal in the center of the room and framing the sides with tile on the square.

- Create a lit niche in the wall to display a beautiful object. Trim with distressed wood, stone, stucco, tile, or Venetian plaster.

- Trim the perimeter of skylights with crown molding that conceals xenon festoon lighting to create an after-dark romantic glow.

- Use "Meshed Stone" to cover walls for a unique texture. To "mesh stone," select a 12 × 12" stone tile, such as a marble, cut it into 1 × 1" squares, then mount the squares randomly on nylon mesh for easy installation.

- Install indirect or dimmable lighting that is easy on the eyes for bathers reclining or relaxing in the tub.

Two of the many faces of concrete are shown here. That's right: both the typical square floor tile shown at left and the custom pattern shown at right are concrete.

No longer drab or boring in the least, concrete can be colored with a huge variety of pigments, cast into virtually any shape imaginable, and given any finish from matte to glossy. A well-sealed concrete floor is both stain and water resistant, but it can be quite heavy. Concrete floors require careful maintenance and may require additional structural support. If you're considering concrete in your bathroom, talk with your designer or supplier first, and make sure you understand the structural support that's necessary as well as the nature of concrete and the care it requires.

Floor-warming Systems

Imagine stepping from a warm shower onto an equally comfortable floor. It can happen in any weather if you install a floor warming system beneath the floor covering in your bathroom.

Floor-warming systems are an affordable luxury. Systems that rely on warm water to heat the floor typically require professional installation; other systems employ electric resistance wires that heat up when energized, similar to an electric blanket, and can be installed by confident do-it-yourselfers. Either way, the system is installed beneath the floor covering and wired to a thermostat to control the temperature and a timer that can turn it on and off automatically.

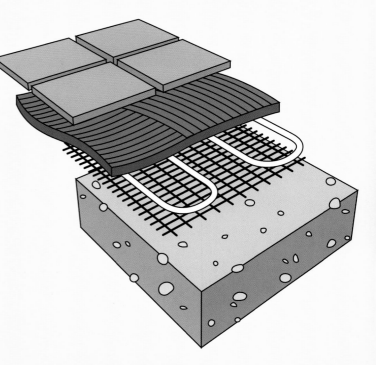

Medicine cabinets tucked into wall cavities provide the kind of storage that can be missing in bathrooms without vanity cabinets.

Painted quarter-round eases the transition between the floor and walls.

Wooden bases lift the pedestals into position to shield the plumbing from view and protect users from hot water supply pipes.

Protect wood floors with high-quality, water-resistant sealer.

Wood covers all the bases in this bathroom—floors, walls, and ceilings. To provide contrast, each surface is treated to a different finish. Stained planks warm the floor; painted car-siding boards embrace the walls; pickled tongue-and-groove paneling highlights the ceiling.

Wood brings beauty to a bathroom, but it also brings potential problems—chiefly water damage. Some woods, such as teak, redwood, and mahogany, are naturally water resistant, but other varieties tend to expand and contract as temperatures and humidity levels fluctuate, which can lead to warping.

To safely use wood in a bathroom, make sure every inch is protected with a high-quality, water-resistant sealer, conscientiously use the vent fan when showering or bathing, and wipe up spills and splashes quickly and thoroughly.

Ceilings

The ceilings in most bathrooms are constructed with a drywall base and covered with paint or wallcovering, a good alternative, but not the only one. No, the limit for bathrooms ceilings is only a little short of the sky itself. Ceilings can be covered in wood, tile, or metal; they can play host to decorative beams or even trompe l'oile murals. In short, any material that's attractive, moisture resistant, and able to be structurally supported can be used on a bathroom ceiling.

(left) Choose a ceiling material that supports the theme of the room. Here, tongue-and-groove paneling and timber beams complement the log-cabin ambience.

Wood requires protection anywhere in a bathroom, even a ceiling. Although it's unlikely that water will be splashed up onto the ceiling very often, warm, moist air will rise to the ceiling every time the tub or shower are used. A yearly coat of sealer keeps a wood ceiling beautiful and carefree.

(right) When circumstances call for moisture resistance, think ceramic tile. Other materials might fail here, but the ceramic tile ceiling, walls, and floor of this luxurious bathroom withstand even the copious amounts of moisture released by the steam room and large, sunken whirlpool tub.

Strong architecture requires subtle treatments. Here, cream paint on flat-finished drywall encourages the interplay of shadows along the dramatic angles of the ceiling and walls.

Feel free to be a perfectionist when it comes to a flat finish on drywall ceilings—skillful craftsmanship and real attention to detail is required to make a ceiling like this look its best.

Wallpaper draws the ceiling down to the walls, creating a more intimate feeling in this airy bathroom.

Good ventilation is essential in wallpapered bathrooms—excessive moisture can loosen the adhesive and cause the seams and edges to peel up. Powder rooms, bathrooms with standard tubs rather than whirlpools or showers, and rooms with operable windows are good candidates for wallpapered ceilings or walls. A wallpapered bathroom, as any other, needs a ventilation fan rated to handle the square footage of the room, and family members need to use the fan when bathing or showering.

*Skylights bring
light and energy
to a bathroom.*

Many designers say that skylights are the best thing you can do for a ceiling. Most suggest units that can be opened and closed with remote controls, feature low-E glass, and have several modes of light control.

Take care when placing skylights: In hot climates, avoid south- or west-facing skylights or choose units that can be shaded in the afternoon.

In this light-colored ceiling, light from the opposing skylights is multiplied as it bounces between the skylights, window, ceiling, and walls.

In this windowless bathroom, skylights contribute lovely and much appreciated light. Be especially careful with the placement of inoperable skylights—north or east exposures and shaded areas are the best choices.

CHAPTER 2

Storage and Display

Remember the old saying that you can never be too rich or too thin? That opinion is—and always has been—debatable, but this much is true: Most of us can never have enough bathroom storage. It takes a whole lot of lotions and potions to maintain the youthful appearance to which so many of us aspire.

According to people who research these sorts of things, the average American woman applies 33 products to her face and body each morning before leaving the house. You read that right—*thirty-three* products. Add the products used by a spouse or partner and a child or two, and you're looking at 40 to 50 containers competing for space in the bathroom. And that's for an average family—high-maintenance folks have an even larger array.

And so we come to the subject of storage, which unleashes a series of questions. How many cabinets do you need, and should they be built-in or freestanding? Closed cabinets or open shelves? Is a pedestal sink workable or do you need a vanity?

Only you can answer these important questions, but we're here to help. We invite you to read through this chapter with an open mind. Take notes about what you find interesting and attractive, then spend some time thinking about your family's habits and routines. The best storage solutions are ones that meet your specific needs and suit your personal taste.

Cabinets

Whether you're adding or remodeling a bathroom, cabinetry is one of the most important investments you'll make. Some elements—floor coverings, paint and wall coverings, and so forth—change along with design trends. (Experts estimate that bathrooms are freshened, on average, every seven to ten years.) Cabinetry, however, has a very long useful life and is likely to remain in place for many years.

If you're in the process of a remodeling project and your cabinets work well, consider painting or refacing them. Paint is an option only for wood cabinets, but both wood and laminate cabinets can be refaced by installing new cabinet doors, drawer fronts, and matching veneer on face frames and cabinet ends.

Ready-to-assemble cabinets are available through home centers and furnishings retailers. Typically offered in set sizes, standard pieces are configured to fit the room.

Stock cabinets, available through home centers, are offered in a range of standard sizes, usually in 3" increments. A limited variety of door styles and colors can be purchased off the shelf or delivered within a few days.

Semi-custom cabinets are manufactured in hundreds of standard sizes, finishes, and styles. You can buy these cabinets through home centers, kitchen designers, and contractors. Following a plan that you or you and a designer have created, your cabinets are built to order according to the manufacturer's standard specifications.

Custom cabinets are built by a custom manufacturer or by a cabinet shop. In either case, you can expect high-quality materials and workmanship as well as luxurious details and accessories. You can also expect to pay a price for these luxuries.

Bathroom cabinets should meet your needs. Consider who uses the bathroom, how and when, and plan storage that works for your life. Here, a combination of doors, drawers, and open shelves store toiletries and grooming essentials for the two adults who use the room, typically one at a time.

More users should equal more cabinets. This owner's suite includes plenty of room for both of the homeowners to get ready for the day without bumping into one another. In addition to plenty of shelves, the cabinets include a tower of drawers that could store lingerie, pajamas, and other clothing items necessary at the beginning or end of the day.

Changes in the profile and counter height keep this long line of cabinets from becoming ungainly. The furniture legs on the vanities give them the appearance of individual pieces of custom furniture, a nice touch in a large piece like this.

Words to the Wise

On framed cabinets, the exposed edges of the cases are covered with flat (face) frames. The doors may be set into the frames or overlay them; the hinges are attached to the frames and the doors. Framed cabinets require more materials but often are less exacting to build than frameless. They are preferable in historic or traditional-style homes.

On frameless cabinets, the exposed edges are covered with edge banding and the doors cover nearly the entire case. The door hinges are attached to the doors and the sides or ends of the cases. Frameless cabinets require less material but can be more time consuming to build than framed. The structure allows for wider doors and better accessibility.

The main goal for storage in a bathroom—or any other room, for that matter—is to keep things near their point of use. Simple. Hair dryers should be housed near mirrors; towels near the shower, tub, and sinks; bubble bath near the tub. You get the idea.

The trick to planning efficient storage is first to figure out what is used and where, then to decide how and where those things will be stored. Consider placing pull-out shelves and drawers, hampers, and trash cans behind closed doors. Don't underestimate the importance of well-placed towel bars and robe hooks. These small details play a large role in the convenience level of daily living.

To be convenient for an average-sized person, toiletries should be stored within 15 to 48" of the floor.

Make use of the space behind false fronts by exchanging them for tip-out drawers where you can store toothpaste, dental floss, and other small personal-care items.

Bold and beautiful, the deep stain on these cabinets creates an intimate feeling that might otherwise be missing in this large, light-filled bathroom. Plenty of cabinet space, drawers, and open shelves are arranged to suit the homeowners' needs.

Accessories and other decorative items are displayed at eye level. These shallow shelves would also be good places to store towels or clear containers of beauty supplies, such as cotton swabs, cotton balls, and sponges.

Place towel bars or hooks within 12" of sinks, tubs, and showers.

The NKBA recommends 20" of clearance from the centerline of a lavatory to a side wall.

The generous space between these sinks leaves plenty of counter space around both sinks. The NKBA recommends 36" from centerline to centerline of double sinks.

Having a place for everything simplifies daily life.

Ergonomic experts tell us that the most useful storage space is between hip and shoulder height, yet the majority of bathroom storage is tucked under sinks and countertops. Not in this bathroom. Here, the double sinks are separated not merely by counter space, but by a shallow, pantry-like cabinet. Stored in an upper cabinet, grooming necessities can be reached without bending or stooping, which many of us appreciate first thing in the morning.

Trim molding surrounds the vanity area, framing it within the tall walls and high ceiling.

Brass door knobs and drawer pulls are coordinated with the brass fittings and accessories.

Simple molding complements the design of the raised panel doors and drawers as well as the elegance of the molding on the doors and walls of the room.

Cosmetics and medications need to be stored in cool, dark, dry places.

Oddly enough, medicine cabinets rarely fit that description. In fact, medicine cabinets can be warm, humid environments. Think about it: they're often recessed, almost always above or adjacent to a sink, and typically surrounded by lights. Definitely not ideal. Reserve other, more appropriate places for your cosmetics and medications, and make sure medications are stored securely.

If there are children in your home, medications as well as cleaning supplies need to be completely inaccessible to them. Putting these items up out of reach isn't enough, either. Children have a way of reaching whatever captures their attention, and childproof caps aren't always childproof. Include a locking cabinet or fit a cabinet door or drawer with secure safety latches. Remember: lives depend on this.

*Design*Wise

Pat Currier, CKD
Currier Kitchens & Baths
Amherst, New Hampshire

- There no longer seems to be a standard height for bathroom vanities. While 31" is typical, some master baths are implementing standard-height kitchen cabinets at 36". When selecting bathroom vanities, find a height that's comfortable for you and your family.

- Major manufacturers have begun using better products to treat vanities for the moist environments of bathrooms. Catalyzed-conversion varnishes and Thermofoil—a PVC film applied to fiberboard that imitates the look of paint— make cabinets downright water resistant.

- Function may be the most important consideration when selecting vanities and countertops. That vision of a beautiful marble counter topping an antique table may be perfect for a guest powder room, but impractical for daily grooming. Assess how your bathroom is most used, then look for materials that are best suited for that application.

- Laminate countertops are still the most cost-effective countertop material, and are now offered in a wider variety of colors and patterns than ever before. Many modern laminates also are available with scratch-resistant finishes.

Accentuate the positive.
Sections of cabinets unfurl against the curve of this wall, topped by a wood backsplash that emphasizes the room's graceful shape.

The elegant, curved trim on the backsplash complements the contrasting tones of the wood countertop. All the wood in this bathroom has been treated to high-quality sealers to protect it against water damage. Sealers of this sort need to be reapplied yearly in order to maintain their protection.

*Idea*Wise

It just can't be done: You can never have too much storage in a bathroom. Especially in small bathrooms, take every opportunity to add storage.

Frame an opening into a partition—or non-load-bearing wall—and trim it out with window casings.

Have glass shelves cut to fit the opening and install them on small cleats attached to the sides of the opening.

If privacy is an issue, fill the shelves with plants and other decorative items to block the view.

There's no rule that the main storage facilities have to surround the sink. Here, a simple tapered column supports the sink, which is flanked by a sleek line of drawers and a simple bench.

Extra storage is tucked into every possible space in this gleaming bathroom. One wall of the tub surround is converted to storage space by open shelves and cubby holes that hold wash cloths, soaps, candles, and cosmetic and beauty supplies. Nearby, hand and bath towels are kept fresh and dust free behind a glass door, and other, less attractive supplies are hidden by a raised-panel door.

Accessibility

Creating an accessible bathroom is mostly a matter of planning and consideration, which can make a bathroom more attractive and comfortable for the whole family. Consider these suggestions as you plan your bathroom cabinets and countertops:

• Add pull-down hardware to upper shelves (such as those in wall-mounted cabinets or medicine cabinets) to bring items into reach for seated people or those with limited mobility. Or, mount shelves or a medicine cabinet on the side of the sink rather than behind it to minimize reaching.

• Use fold-away doors, remove face frames on base cabinets, or install roll-out base cabinets to gain clear space beneath countertops.

• Provide clear space that is 29" high by 32 to 36" wide under sinks and lowered sections of countertop so seated users can comfortably reach the vanity.

• Vary the heights of the countertops to serve both standing and seated users.

• Conceal a pop-up step stool behind the toe-kick of a cabinet for the convenience of children and other small people.

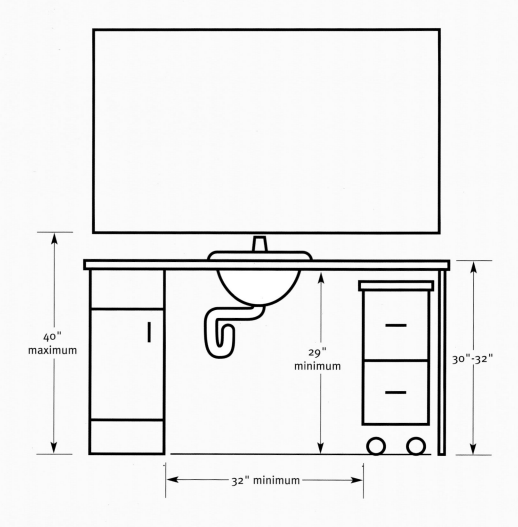

Accessibility doesn't have to announce itself.

This attractive, comfortable bathroom has been designed for maximum accessibility and efficiency for everybody.

Roll-out base cabinets provide seating space without sacrificing storage.

Easy-to-grip C-shaped pulls make drawers more accessible.

Bars attached to the front of the counter-tops allow seated users to pull themselves into position—and hold towels right where they're needed.

Insulated pipes protect seated users from burns.

Placing the sink toward the front of the counter makes it easier to reach. (There should be no more than 21" from the front of the counter to the back of the sink.)

Including countertops and sinks at different heights creates accessible space for all users. Comfortable heights range from 32 to 43" for standing users and 30 to 34" for seated users.

In major remodeling projects or new construction, decide on locations and sizes for the towel bars early in the process so blocking can be installed before the drywall is hung.

Candles, bathing salts and a basket containing loofas, brushes, and other exfoliators rest on the ledge of the luxurious whirlpool, waiting for the next bather.

Teak, a durable hardwood, is at home in moist environments, such as bathrooms. This bench holds clothing and other items while family members bathe, and makes a great place to sit while changing clothes.

Towels, sponges, even soaps and candles are stored where they're used in this relaxed atmosphere.

By the way, if you haven't considered one before, now's the time: a towel warmer may be the ultimate luxury. These days, towel warmers can be found at surprisingly reasonable prices. Some are hard-wired into an available electrical circuit; others simply plug into a receptacle. Either way, you're in for a treat. Who wouldn't love wrapping themselves in a warm, fluffy towel on a cold day?

Transform necessities into accessories by storing them in plain sight.

Large, bulky, or unattractive items are hidden behind closed doors in the vanity cabinets.

Slightly obscured behind textured glass doors, common objects such as a hand mirror, pottery, and towels become decorative pieces in their own right.

Displaying towels attractively isn't exactly fine art, but there is a trick to it. For each stack, fold all the towels in the same manner and to the same size, then stack them with all the folds facing the same direction. This might sound trivial, but try it. Details like this transform ordinary things into extraordinary displays.

White on white on white might have become formless without the black border that defines the perimeter of the room and emphasizes the shape of the sink and storage pieces.

(above) A console table and sink can be nestled between stacks of drawers. In drawer stacks like these, store things according to how often you use them—place those used most often in the top drawer, least often in the bottom.

Take advantage of any open space around the sink. Here, a generous storage piece tucked between the sink and tub holds daily supplies and sports a towel ring for the sink.

Console-table sinks offer no real storage, which can present problems. If you love the style but think you can't sacrifice the storage offered by a vanity, think again. You may have more options than you first realize.

Make sure wood accessories are protected by water-resistant finishes.

Designers suggest storing towels within 12" of sinks, tubs, and showers. If your bathroom doesn't meet this guideline, fill in with accessories. Here, a simple set of wood shelves stores towels within reach of both the shower and the tub.

Countertops

Today's bathroom countertops can be anything from glass to wood to synthetics to concrete to natural stone. Ceramic tile also remains a favorite. Each material has its own strengths and weaknesses and each comes at a particular price. Some combine fantastic looks with fantastic prices; others combine reasonable prices with limitations regarding edge treatment and sink options. It's all a balancing act. In this case, you're balancing appearance, performance, and price.

It isn't important to choose a material that follows the trends of the moment, it's important to choose one that meets the needs of your family for each particular bathroom. The materials you'd choose for countertops in a family bath or children's bathroom may be quite different from what you'd select for a powder room near an entertainment area, for example.

It's also important to select countertops that complement other materials in the room. Generally, it's best to select your cabinets and flooring materials, then choose materials, colors, and textures for your countertops.

Remember that with most materials, matte finishes hide scratches better than glossy ones, and textured finishes are interesting but can be hard to keep clean.

Wood molding or special nosing covers the edges of laminate counters and adds a nice sense of style.

Solid-core laminate has color all the way through the body, which eliminates that issue. Solid-core is, however, more expensive and typically isn't available in as wide an array of colors and textures.

Plastic laminate has been a popular choice for decades because it's inexpensive, durable, and easy to maintain. Made of several layers of paper impregnated with phenolic resin and bonded by heat and pressure, the laminate itself is highly water resistant, but the substrate beneath isn't, so seams and sink cutouts have to be sealed thoroughly. The kraft-paper core of standard plastic laminate creates a dark line that can be seen on the edges.

Plastic laminate countertops scorch fairly easily—be careful with curling irons and other grooming appliances. It also can be scratched and chipped, but that typically isn't much of a problem in bathrooms.

Corners should be rounded for safety.

Solid-surface materials are one of the most popular countertop materials on the market. They're entirely water resistant and resist heat, marks, and scratches. The color goes all the way through, so minor scratches and marks easily can be sanded or polished away.

Solid-surface materials can be cut and shaped, which means they can be formed into interesting contours and given elaborate edge profiles. Here, an octagonal countertop crowns a vanity island. The malleability of solid-surface materials made it possible to cut the unusual countertop and form a pleasing, rounded profile on its edges.

The chief disadvantage of solid-surface material is the cost. Depending on the style, dimensions, and edge treatments you select, these countertops can be quite expensive. Only you can evaluate their value.

Storage towers surround this unique curved double-vanity countertop. As with all integral solid-surface sinks, the transitions between the countertop and sinks are seamless, despite the shift in color.

Solid-surface materials can be shaped to fit almost any situation.

The availability of thinner materials gives you endless options for backsplashes and surrounds.

Holes can be drilled to accommodate any faucet style.

No seams to trap dirt or grime.

Tile is impervious to water and stains, but the grout that fills the joints can be susceptible to damage from everyday wear and tear. Using epoxy grout reduces staining, mildew, and other damage on countertops and backsplashes. Epoxy grout is easy to use and easy to clean after installation.

The grout—but not the tile—should be sealed with a good-quality sealer once a year.

Tile is a perennial favorite for countertops and backsplashes because it's available in a vast range of sizes, styles, and colors; it's durable and can be repaired; some tile—not all—is reasonably priced.

Floor tile is the best choice for most countertops because it's harder and more durable than wall tile. Several types of tile, including glazed ceramic and porcelain tile as well as glass tile, make excellent countertops.

Mosaic glass tile covers this luminous countertop. Surrounding the sink with a contrasting color customizes the counter and gives it an extra splash of personality.

Speaking of splash, the backsplash here combines the two colors from the countertop with wavy liners, resulting in an all together pleasing arrangement.

One thing to keep in mind when choosing tile, especially small tile such as these, is that the many grout joints can create an uneven surface. This is less of an issue with large tile because they cover more space and, therefore, have fewer joints.

(right) Glass reveals countertops with great style. Here, a vessel sink rests atop a custom glass top. Installing a glass console table is another way to add glass counters to a bath.

To make a countertop, tempered glass—typically between ½ and 1" thick—is cut to size and then the edges are rounded and polished. These countertops are more practical than you might first think. Glass is nonporous, so it's stain proof and sanitary, the one-piece countertops have no dirt-and-grim catching seams, and tempered glass can support a surprising amount of weight.

Glass counters can be smooth, textured, etched, sandblasted, or patterned. Texture hides the surface scratches that glass can develop.

A custom glass top added to a vanity, such as this one, requires support beneath the cabinet.

(left) Concrete countertops can be formed into shapes from sleek to fanciful, such as the "banjo" vanity here. It requires adequate support and regular maintenance.

Daily cleaning is simple; most manufacturers recommend mild, nonabrasive, non-ammoniated soap. Regular maintenance is not quite as simple: concrete must be sealed initially and the sealer must be reapplied periodically.

Before committing to concrete countertops, discuss specific care recommendations with the manufacturer or fabricator. Make sure you're comfortable with the ongoing commitment required by these outstanding countertops.

Natural stone enjoys tremendous popularity for good reason: It's elegant, most stone is easy to care for, and it's undeniably durable. Different varieties of stone have different characteristics and care requirements. Stone countertops give you the option of using undermount sinks, which have to be surrounded by finished, watertight edges.

With advances in protective sealers, wood has moved into the bathroom in new and surprising places, including countertops. Traditionally, most species of wood haven't mixed well with water, so the idea may be somewhat counterintuitive, but today's sealers make it practical as well as possible.

Here, thick planks have been shaped into a marquis-shaped countertop tailored to fit the curved wall that helps support it.

CHAPTER 3

Fixtures

W hat is it about warm water that so soothes our souls? After a good cry or before any major life transaction, we head to the sink to wash our faces, brush our teeth, and prepare ourselves for what lies ahead. And although a good shower or bath won't cure the common cold or solve life's major mysteries, we humans seem to feel better about it all after a good soak.

And so we must have sinks and tubs and showers suited to the purpose. And don't forget the toilet and possibly a bidet. Small wonder that bathrooms have grown larger—they had to in order to house our ever-larger array of fixtures. In the 1950s, the average bathroom was no bigger than 5 × 7 feet; today's master baths are often twice that size.

If you have the space, the question then becomes how to fill it. A toilet is, of course, a necessity, but what about a bidet? What is it and do you need or even want one? Is a whirlpool tub the ultimate luxury for you, or would a mammoth, multiple-head shower better suit your lifestyle and proclivities? How many sinks do you need and what style should they be?

No one can answer these questions for you, but this chapter showcases a range of available options and provides information to help you answer them for yourself. Maybe you should read it while soaking in the tub. . . .

With so many options available, there's no reason to settle for hum-drum fixtures. Start with the basic realities—the dimensions of the room and the current locations of the plumbing—and let your imagination run as far as your space and budget allow.

If you're remodeling and plan to use an existing countertop, make sure you have the measurements of the countertop and cutout with you when shopping for a new sink. You can choose a sink that is the same size or larger as long as the plumbing remains in the same location.

A coatrack holds towels within reach of both the tub and shower.

A sliding showerhead lets users adjust the shower to varying heights.

Plumbing rises from the floor to serve this freestanding tub. Placing the faucets at the side of this tub allows bathers to rest comfortably against the end while enjoying the view.

Glass walls and doors have to be wiped down or squeegeed after every shower to keep them looking their best.

Vitreous china sinks are durable and nonporous, and easy to clean. Deep bowls reduce splashing.

The sinks, tubs, and showers in a bathroom should present a unified—but not necessarily matching—face to the world. Here, a contemporary glass shower sits among traditional-style fixtures and accessories, letting the room's abundant light move freely. A white-on-white color scheme, accented by deep wood tones, unifies the eclectic mix.

Sinks

Sinks are the most used fixture in any bathroom. Think about it: According to experts, the average person visits the bathroom six to eight times a day, and each of those visits includes (or certainly should) the obligatory trip to the sink; toothpaste commercials as well as our very own dentists encourage us to brush our teeth at least twice a day; we wash our hands before and after meals. You get the idea—sinks are part of our everyday lives, and they ought to be practical to use, attractive to look at, and accessible to every member of the family.

Many sinks, such as this one, are sold with pre-drilled holes for a faucet. Select a faucet that fits the hole pattern of the sink you've chosen—in this case, a single hole model.

Caulk seals the joint between the sink and countertop, preventing water damage.

Easy to install and often reasonably priced, self-rimming is the most popular style of sink. Here, a simple white sink is transformed into a striking piece with the addition of a unique ceramic faucet.

Free-standing sinks work in combination with wall-mounted faucets. With its basin resting atop a fanciful stand, this sink contributes high style as well as simple function. Lovely as it is, a sink such as this is best suited to a powder room or other lightly used bathroom rather than one in which multiple users get ready for each day.

Words to the Wise

Sinks often are categorized according to how and where they are installed.

Vanity-mounted sinks are available in a range of styles:

Self-rimming sinks have rolled edges that rest directly on the countertop. This is typically the least expensive type of sink as well as the easiest to install. The drawback is that the joint between the sink and countertop attracts dirt and has to be cleaned regularly.

Flush-mounted sinks are recessed into the counter to sit flush with the surface. They blend nicely with countertops and are easy to keep clean. (A variation, tile-in sinks, is made to be used with tile countertops.)

Undermount sinks fit below the countertop. The edges of the countertop are exposed in this arrangements, so those edges have to be finished and watertight. For this reason, undermount sinks are often used with solid-surface or stone countertops.

Integral sinks are molded basins that are actually part of the countertops. Stainless steel and solid-surface countertops often include integral sinks,

which are attractive, virtually seamless, and very expensive. Minor damage can usually be buffed out of these materials, but major damage means the whole unit has to be replaced, an expensive proposition.

Vessel sinks are reminiscent of the wash basins of years gone by. Each of these sinks rests above a small cut-out opening that is covered by the base of the vessel. They require surface- or wall-mounted faucets.

Vanity-top sinks rest above the countertop, appearing to be free-standing.

Wall-hung sinks are—as the name suggests—mounted directly to the wall at a comfortable height. They're highly useful in small bathrooms and in bathrooms designed for accessibility. Some models come with decorative shields to conceal the plumbing. Wall-hung sinks typically require special blocking between wall studs for structural support.

Pedestal and Free-standing sinks are attached to the wall and given additional support by the decorative bases on which they rest.

Pedestal sinks typically lack counterspace, but the generous deck of this sink provides a bit of room to work with as one prepares for the day. Hand towels rest on built-in towel bars and other sundries and supplies wait in a pantry-like cabinet.

Accessibility

To be accessible to seated users, a sink should be installed within 21" of the front edge of a countertop. When that's not possible, consider mounting the faucet controls at the side of the sink rather than the back. Or, choose a design that juts out past the counter's edge, which provides easy access from a seated position.

If you're shopping for an accessible sink, choose a style that's shallower at the front and deeper at the drain. When installing it, provide clear space that is 29" high by 32 to 36" wide beneath the sink and a lowered section of countertop.

*Idea*Wise

Vessel sinks are all the rage, but prices for some of those vessels are raging, too. If you want high style without the high prices, transform a simple waterproof vessel into a sink.

Cut a hole in the center of a vessel such as a laquerware, glass, or pottery bowl. Use a rotary cutter, a carbide bit, and a deft touch to cut the hole. If you're using laquerware, add several coats of laquer, letting it dry between coats.

Sandwich plumber's putty between the bowl and a drain body, and you've got a custom-made vessel sink on your hands.

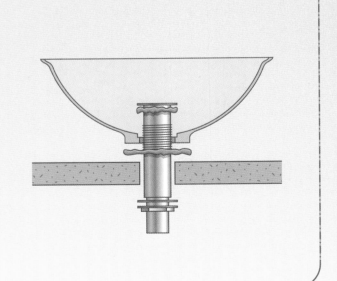

Make sure there is at least 30" between double sinks, measured from centerline to centerline.

Who decided double sinks have to be identical?

If you can't decide between two sink styles, don't fret—choose both. Here, a raised vessel rests beside its counterpart, an under-mounted bowl. Both sinks and the countertops are solid-surface material, an elegant, practical material that can be fabricated into an almost infinite variety of shapes and sizes.

Like solid-surface countertops, solid-surface sinks are durable, easy to maintain, and clean up like a dream. If a sink becomes discolored, fill it with warm water, a little laundry detergent, and a small amount of chlorine bleach. Let the water soak until it's cool, then rinse the sink thoroughly.

Wall-mounted sinks are practical in bathrooms where accessibility is an issue or where space is at a premium. Here, a creamy wall-hung sink floats like a cloud against a sky blue wall, the supply pipes and drain concealed within the wall. Concealment isn't always possible, so plumbing shrouds are available to match most wall-hung sinks.

Wall-hung sinks require a fair amount of support. In major remodeling projects, decide on the location and height of the sinks early, and add blocking for wall-hung sinks before the drywall is hung. If the drywall is already in place, it's possible to cut away a section and add the necessary support.

Console-table sinks combine the space saving ways of pedestal sinks with a little bit of counterspace and a whole lot of style. A console table consists of a ledge surrounding a sink supported by the wall and at least two legs.

Console tables are available in many shapes, styles and colors. Some are offered with optional detachable shelves, towel rings, plumbing shrouds—even romantic fabric skirting.

Sinks can be installed in furniture pieces that have
been adapted for the purpose. The chief require-
ment for this type of transformation is stability—
in particular, a well supported countertop.
With that in place, any style of sink can be added.

This vintage sideboard has been outfitted with an undermount sink and a marble countertop and backsplash. To
accomplish this transformation, typically the top of the piece is
removed. The sink is securely attached to the countertop, often with mounting strips, then the countertop is installed with
corner braces and blocking.

Nontraditional materials find homes in today's bathrooms.

Stainless steel is. . .well. . .stainless, a fine attribute for a bathroom sink. Traditionally, stainless steel has been used more for kitchen sinks than for bathrooms, but current trends are changing that. After all, stainless steel hides dirt well; it's also durable and easy to clean. To produce this stain and corrosion resistant material, manufacturers combine stainless steel, chromium, and nickel.

The mirror finish on this console sink has to be treated gently—it scratches easily—so a sink like this would be most appropriate in a powder room or guest bath.

As long as holes can be drilled in the surrounding countertop, you can combine any style of faucet with an undermount sink.

Undermount sinks can be used only with countertops that have substantial waterproof edges, such as natural stone and solid-surface materials.

If your heart is set on a stainless steel sink in a heavily used bathroom, choose a satin finish. It doesn't show fingerprints or scratches as easily, and minor scratches can be buffed out with a scouring pad. Here, a stainless steel undermount sink is paired with a slate countertop, an interesting combination for the rustic setting.

Clearly elegant, glass sinks are surprisingly practical as well. They're scratch resistant, easy to clean, and—despite their fragile appearance—strong and durable. Even rapid changes in water temperature don't phase glass sinks.

Air bubbles that formed during the casting process give spun glass a pebbly surface that makes the sink interesting and inviting. And although the sink shown here is clear, colored glass is widely available.

To keep glass sinks looking their best, wipe them dry after use. Even when you're careful, spots left by the minerals in hard water are tough to avoid. If you don't have a water softener, add one. It will reduce the mineral content of the water and substantially reduce spotting.

Yes, that really is a wood sink and tub. The natural tones of the wood sink and tub positively glow against the deep green marble of the countertop, tub surround, and floor. It's not all that surprising—wood boats have been around for centuries. Properly maintained, this wood sink and tub will remain beautiful for a lifetime.

Bathtubs

Hip magazines and books continually preach about the restorative powers of warm water. From their pages, self-help gurus exhort us to wash our aches and pains—along with our cares and woes—down the drain as often as possible. For that you need a comfortable, attractive bathtub in a size, shape, and material that suits your bathroom and your family.

As you evaluate your options regarding the tub itself, there are other issues to consider. The first is size: You have to get the tub into the room and into position. Then, there are issues of structural support, plumbing, and—for a spa tub—wiring. And, no matter what your age or physical abilities, it's important to consider safety and accessibility when it comes to bathtubs.

The profile of the integral apron lends a sophisticated air to this classic tub.

The splash zone on alcove walls should be covered in water-resistant material, such as this elegant combination of marble and painted wood.

Alcove tubs are the most common type of tub for family bathrooms. These tubs are designed to fit into niches finished by walls on two or—more commonly—three sides. They're sold either with an integral or separate "apron" covering the exposed side of the tub.

Here, the tub is tucked into a three-sided alcove beneath a window. Having a window above a tub can be delightful—it provides wonderful light and ventilation—but when it's at the business end of the tub it complicates the placement of plumbing. In this alcove, that problem was neatly solved by adding a bumped-out wall to house the plumbing.

Alcove tubs with only one side apron are sold as either "left-hand" or "right-hand" models, depending on the location of the predrilled drain and overflow holes in the tub. To determine which type you need, face into the alcove and determine whether the tub drain is (or will be) on your right or left.

Tub and shower combinations pack a lot of options into small spaces. Here, a one-piece module includes both a tub and shower. The walls of the tub surround were specially molded to give the appearance of ceramic tile and to provide space for towels and other bathing necessities.

To prevent scalding, tub and shower control valves must be pressure balanced, thermostatic mixing, or a combination of those types.

Words to the Wise

Tubs are manufactured from a variety materials, each with its own set of advantages and disadvantages.

Fiberglass is an inexpensive, lightweight material available in many colors. It is easily molded, so tub units can be formed to include seats, grab bars, and other conveniences. The surface of fiberglass scratches easily and its color fades over time.

Acrylic, like fiberglass, can be molded into just about any size and shape. Unlike fiberglass, however, the color runs through the entire substance rather than just the surface coat, making it less likely to fade or develop scratches.

Enameled steel tubs are shaped from sheets of steel and coated with a baked-on enamel similar to that of cast-iron tubs. However, the enamel layer usually is thin and susceptible to chipping. In addition, enameled steel doesn't retain heat and tends to be noisy. When buying an enameled steel tub, make sure it has an undercoating designed to muffle sound and retain heat.

Cast iron is the toughest material available for tubs. The iron is cast into a tub shape then coated with a baked-on enamel that is relatively thick (1/16"), resulting in a richly colored finish. The enamel is strong, durable, and very resistant to chips, scratches, and stains. The cast iron itself is almost impervious to dents and cracks. Cast iron is just about indestructible, and it's also heavy—a standard tub weighs between 300 and 400 pounds. Often the floor framing must be reinforced to support the additional weight. Cast iron is used most commonly for claw-foot and other free-standing tubs.

Deck-mounted tubs and whirlpools rest on the subfloor and are surrounded by custom-built decks or platforms. Here, tile covers the deck and surrounding walls, creating a spa atmosphere.

Typically, deck-mounted and platform tubs have a larger capacity than standard tubs and a more luxurious feel. Although the tubs themselves are priced much like alcove tubs, the construction of the deck or platform can add a significant amount to the total cost.

Before adding a tub configuration like this in a remodeling project, make sure the floor will support its weight. Replace existing floor joists beneath the tub if they're damaged, too small, or too far apart. Generally, you'll need to add support under the tub area if the current joists are 2 × 10 or smaller, or if they're more than 16" apart. If you have questions about support issues, contact a building inspector or professional contractor.

Light fixtures above tubs must be vapor-proof and carry a UL rating for wet areas.

This deck-mounted tub is surrounded by ocean-blue tile and a glass-block shower in a serene dream of a bathroom. Classic cream-colored fixtures are combined with water-colored tones in a number of textures to form a decorating scheme that will remain fresh and inviting for decades.

For many people, a spa tub is the ultimate bathroom luxury. And while these tubs are undeniably relaxing and enjoyable, adding one to a bathroom is not entirely simple.

Before you choose a spa tub, talk with your designer, contractor, or a local building inspector to make sure you understand all the ramifications of that choice. Once you have a firm grasp on the requirements and expenses involved, if those tiny bubbles are still calling you, go for it!

Words to the Wise

Hot tubs recirculate water alone.

Whirlpool tubs pump a combination of air and water through a series of jets. They require access to the pumps and other plumbing as well as frequent and thorough cleaning.

Air jet tubs pump warm water into the tub. Water doesn't circulate through the pipes, so there's no issue of standing water in the pipes and no need for additional plumbing access.

If bathing avec deux is what you have in mind, choose a large-capacity tub and place the spout in the middle so both people can relax comfortably against an end. Position the water controls and faucet toward the outside edge of the tub at a height of 38 to 48" so the water can be turned on and adjusted before you get into the tub…and after.

Use your imagination: Tubs don't always have to be set into niches or alcoves. Deck-mounted tubs can be set as peninsulas or even stand alone in the center of a room.

The placement of this spa tub in combination with the stunning copper tile surrounding the deck make it the centerpiece of the room. Its extra depth and comforting jets make it a pleasure to own and use.

A spa tub holds 50 to 100 gallons of water, which means you may need a large capacity hot water heater and extra support for the floor.

Adding two faucets lets you fill large-capacity tubs more quickly. High-flow valves have an increased flow rate that speeds up the process, too.

Steps surrounding a tub can be dangerous. Make sure the floor covering is extremely slip resistant.

To get the effect of a sunken tub without the dangers, raise the tub on a platform and surround it with space to walk or sit. Here, the tub is sunk into a generous platform with a spectacular view.

(above) Freestanding tubs can be located any place that can be reached by supply lines and drain lines. Supported by wooden braces, this tub stands in front of a bank of floor-to-ceiling windows, giving bathers a doubly luxurious experience.

(left) The panels and ledge of this handsome, custom-built tub are concrete, a material that's tailor-made for contemporary settings such as this.

Not every bathroom can accommodate such a tub—the weight of the concrete alone requires a substantial amount of support in the floor. In fact, some extremely heavy tubs may not be practical on the second floor of a wood-framed house. Contact a professional contractor or building inspector if you have questions about structural support.

Dropping the ceiling over the tub suggests the intimacy of an enclosure without limiting the space in any way.

Sheer curtains can be drawn to obscure the tub from the rest of the room without completely blocking the light or the view.

(below) Tile and stone can be used to build custom tubs in unusual shapes and sizes. Here, dramatic thick porcelain tile is shaped into a simple but elegant soaking tub.

The floor of a custom-made tub is built with floor mortar (or "deck mud"), and must slope toward the drain a minimum of one-quarter inch for every 12 inches.

*Dollar*Wise

If you love the look of claw-foot tubs but not their prices, go treasure hunting. Many salvage yards and reuse centers carry vintage cast iron tubs at reasonable prices.

The next step is to find a good refinisher. Get a referral from someone you know and trust or contact several references from prospective contractors. A good refinishing job will last for decades, but an incorrectly finished tub can chip within months.

Have the interior of the tub refinished and paint the exterior.

Showers

According to trend watchers and other keepers of home design statistics, elaborate showers have overtaken whirlpools as the luxury-of-choice for today's bathrooms. Many of the people who bought enormous whirlpool tubs in the previous decade found that they simply didn't have the time necessary to fill or clean them adequately. Enter the instant gratification of the luxury shower, today's answer to the age-old cry for "Serenity Now."

Today's showers range from the economical efficiency of a tub and shower combination to the all-out decadence of the total body spa, and everything in between. The best shower for your bathroom is one that fits the space available, your budget, and your lifestyle.

Plumbing in a wet wall like this can supply the shower as well as a sink on the other side of the wall.

The multitude of grout lines in mosaic tile gives it superior slip resistance.

Repeating the design motif here calls attention to the shower's curb and reduces the likelihood of tripping over it.

Mosaic glass tile makes an outstanding shower. Here, tile walls and floors surround the shower, relieving any concern about splashing beyond the open shower. In large showers like this, rubber membrane covers the substrate to improve its water resistance.

Simple tile mosaics provide points of interest within the strong color of this tile shower. The tiled niche and bench make it functional as well as beautiful.

Shower benches offer seating for those who shave in the shower as well as for those who tire easily. Benches should be about 18" high and at least 15" deep.

A sliding shower head like this can be adjusted to the right height for each member of the family.

Water tends to puddle in enclosed spaces. To avoid mildew, wipe niches dry after the day's last shower.

Including a variety of shower-heads at a variety of heights makes a shower convenient and comfortable for everyone in the family.

Something for every body.

Lights inside showers must be vapor-proof and rated for use in wet areas.

Two showerheads produce twice the moisture. The ventilation system must be designed to handle the load.

Glass walls and doors need to be wiped down after each shower to avoid mineral spots and soap scum.

The rimless shower doors have no trim to develop mold or mildew. The wide threshold slants into the shower to direct water toward the drain.

Handheld showers are convenient for people in a hurry as well as children and other smaller users.

Large-capacity showers sometimes require special drains as well as 1" supply pipes.

Rain-head showers produce delightful deluges when you have the time to indulge yourself and to get your hair wet. For most of us though, there are times when we need to get in and out of the shower quickly with as little fuss as possible. Enter the hand-held shower head.

With two rain heads and a generous enclosure, this shower easily accommodates two people. Double showers sometimes can be efficient and they certainly can be fun.

This self-cleaning threshold guides water and soap residue to the sloped clean-out feature where it can be wiped away or naturally channeled to the drain.

Convenient features, such as seats and ledges, are molded into many shower modules. This fiberglass-reinforced acrylic shower module features a high domed ceiling, sculpted ledges, and a removable seat.

Most shower modules are available in one-piece or multi-piece units. One-piece units have no seams and are easy to install, but multi-piece units are easier to maneuver through doorways and up staircases as is often necessary in remodeling projects. Seams should be discreet rather than easily visible and should be designed to create watertight seals after installation.

*Design*Wise

Linda Burkhardt
Kitchens & Baths by Linda
Montauk, NY

SHOWERS:

- A built-in shower seat is essential to any custom shower. It's the perfect place to perch and pedicure!

- Glass tiles, natural stones and handmade ceramics are luxury materials to incorporate in bathroom design. If working on a budget, a little bit of luxury material can go a long way. Consider running a band around the shower, adding color in a niche, or topping off a bath with ceramic crown molding.

- For bathrooms with limited space, consider pedestal sinks with ample surface space for necessities. This maximizes floor space and gives the illusion of a bigger room. For a tailored look, consider sinks or pedestals with a rectangular shape.

SINKS:

- Powder room sinks are a great place to reflect your personal style. Whether it's a vessel sink floating on a stone slab, a hand painted basin perched on a flea-market console, or a minimalist modern pedestal, express yourself!

- When selecting materials, consider white porcelain—it's timeless and always more cost effective than fashion colors.

- Undermounted sinks create a clean and uncluttered look, focusing attention on decorative elements. This high-end detail works well in both contemporary and traditional designs.

TUBS:

- With today's busy lifestyles, a soaking tub in a master suite is a great way to create your own personal spa.

- Tub-shower combinations are commonplace in today's homes. Look beyond shallow standard tubs, and consider those that are deeper and wider. To gain more elbowroom in a typical tub-shower, use a curved shower rod.

Solid-surface material showers are attractive and easy care. Prefabricated models have curved corners and smooth surfaces, which eliminate hard-to-clean crevices and grout lines. These modules are available with built-in shelves and ledges, and can be installed directly over existing tile as long as it's sound and securely attached to the wall material.

Solid-surface panels in ¼ and ⅛" thicknesses can be used to create custom-built showers.

Either way, you get the advantages of solid-surface materials—their finish resists stains and water spotting, cleans up easily, and can be buffed to remove small scratches and stains.

Glass block walls make bright, interesting showers. Here, glass block is combined with tile in a large, innovative shower.

Using a wide opening rather than a door is trendy right now, but may or may not be practical, depending on your family and circumstances. A wide, curbless opening like this makes the shower highly accessible, but the floor beyond the opening must be water- and slip-resistant in order to be safe.

Multi-head shower and body spas require full enclosures and plenty of ventilation. Here, the glass walls and doors extend to the ceiling to contain the warmth as well as the energetic splashing of the water.

Tile protects the ceiling.

Operable windows provide welcome light and ventilation in shower enclosures.

A towel bar or hook should be located within 22" of the shower opening.

Accessible Tubs & Showers

Building an accessible shower is mostly a matter of careful planning and attention to detail. Wide, curbless openings, gently sloping floors, adjustable showerheads, and shower seats combine to create showers that everyone can use and enjoy.

A tile design takes the place of rugs, which present tripping hazards and make it difficult for wheelchairs to maneuver.

(below) An alcove shower with an adjustable height showerhead is comfortable for everyone. The sliding bar can be positioned at heights to fit adults of every size, children, and seated users.

Grab bars help users steady themselves on slippery surfaces and support people transferring to a shower or tub from a wheelchair or walker. Here, brass grab bars match the finish on the door handles, controls, and showerheads.

Universal design specialists and the ADA guidelines suggest placing a horizontal grab bar on the control wall, 24" long and 34 to 38" above the floor. The side wall should include a bar 32 to 48" long and 34 to 38" above the floor.

Grab bars must be attached to studs or installed with anchors rated to support at least 300 pounds each.

Shower doors should open into the room so they can't be blocked by someone who has fallen or otherwise needs assistance.

A seat next to the handheld showerhead is convenient for seated users and people who shave in the shower.

Molded supports hold grab bars securely.

Transfer seats make transferring into and out of the tub easier.

Tub and shower combinations offer accessible bathing options in limited space. Tubs designed for accessibility have slip-resistant bottoms and grab bars placed to support users as they shower or transfer into and out of the tub. Tub/shower modules are available in one- and two-piece units.

FIXTURES

Toilets and Bidets

Toilets probably aren't anyone's favorite topic of conversation, but there's a lot to consider when purchasing and placing a toilet.

First, there's style. One-piece toilets are streamlined and seamless—the tank and bowl are integrated. Two-piece toilets have separate tanks and bowls connected with bolts. They're easier to install but typically more bulky.

Then there's shape. Elongated bowl are more comfortable for adults, but they take up more space than round-front bowls. Round bowls can be easier for small children to use. Compact elongated toilets enable a longer bowl to fit in smaller spaces.

And don't forget flushing systems. Reductions in water flow have reduced the power of the flush, which has spawned a variety of technologies designed to produce clean, quiet flushes.

Finally, there's the big question about placement. Should the toilet (and bidet, if there is one) be open to the rest of the room or have its own compartment? There's no one right answer of course. The best choice depends on the space available, the size and shapes of those who use the bathroom on a regular basis.

A bidet basically is a sit-down washbasin. Some consider bidets more hygienic than toilet paper. For those of you who always wanted to know but were afraid to ask, the user sits over the bowl, facing the faucet to control the spray or fill the bowl with water.

Design standards suggest 18" from the centerline of the toilet to the nearest fixture, wall, or other obstruction.

Gravity-fed, two-piece toilets with taller, thinner tanks have improved flushing power.

One-piece toilets, with their simpler lines, often complement contemporary settings. In bathrooms where space is at a premium, they often can fit under an extension of the vanity counter.

Although two-piece toilets usually are sold without seats, a one-piece toilet often comes with a seat designed to complement the lines of the design of the toilet.

Place a toilet paper holder 8 to 12" in front of the toilet bowl, 26" above the floor

Pressure-assisted toilets like this one can save an average of 2,000 gallons of water a year for a typical family.

For some families, space is enough of a separation between the vanity area and toilet. Here, a large but open area hosts both the toilet and bidet, while the remaining fixtures sit out of the direct line of sight.

For those who prefer a measure of privacy but feel claustrophobic in a small compartment, a partial wall topped by textured glass is an appealing option.

Towel bars make wise use of the space above the toilet without interfering with the user's comfort.

Space-efficient pocket doors slide completely out of view when not needed.

For more modest folks, only a separate compartment is truly comfortable. Here, a translucent sliding door provides privacy without blocking the light.

Bidets typically are placed near a toilet in order to share the plumbing and drain lines. Choose a toilet and bidet from the same design group or at least ones that share complementary design lines in order to coordinate the two.

A bidet requires the same space and clearance as a toilet, approximately 48 × 48" of floor space from the front edge to any wall or fixture. Plumbing codes are quite specific with regard to the placement of toilets and bidets—check with your designer, contractor, or local code before committing to a plan for your bathroom.

The shower, bidet, and sink are collected along a wall in this bathroom and the toilet sits modestly in a separate compartment, a perfectly reasonable set-up.

Horizontal spray bidets, with their directionally adjustable sprays, are better for front side cleaning. Vertical sprays, with water that sprays from the bottom of the fixture or fills the basin from above, are better for back side cleaning.

For the sake of convenience, make sure towels are available near the bidet. Here, separate towel bars serve the shower and bidet and the frame of the console sink holds towels for the sink.

Elevated toilets are comfortable for taller users and those who have difficulty sitting down or rising from a seated position. Here, the toilet is placed on a ledge, effectively elevating it.

Taller toilets, sometimes referred to as "comfort-height" are widely available. These toilets, about as tall as a chair, are comfortable for any average-sized adult. Children and smaller users appreciate standard toilets, which are between 15 and 16" tall.

Grab bars make it safer and easier to use a toilet. ADA guidelines and universal design specialists recommend placing a horizontal bar at one side, between 42" to 12 ft. long, 33 to 36" above the floor. They further recommend a grab bar on the wall behind the toilet, 24" to 6 ft. long, 33 to 36" above the floor.

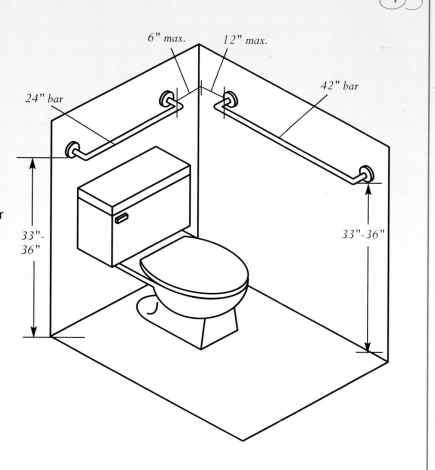

6" max.   12" max.

24" bar

42" bar

33"-36"

33"-36"

CHAPTER 4

Fittings

Fixtures and fittings—faucets, spouts, showerheads, and the like—are sold separately, but they're actually interdependent parts of a whole and have to be compatible with one another. If, for example, you've chosen a single-hole sink, you simply must choose a single-handled faucet. If you've fallen for a large whirlpool, a high-capacity bath valve will fill it faster and help you fit enjoyment of it into your schedule more often.

Compatibility is the most obvious issue when it comes to selecting fittings. Once you know the fitting works with the fixture, you're faced with decisions regarding styles, finishes, and valves, just to name a few. Take some time with these decisions—well-made fittings are virtually indestructible but can be expensive, and some gorgeous pieces require more care than you may be willing to invest. The best fitting is one that suits your bathroom, your budget, and your lifestyle.

Throughout this chapter you'll see fittings in a range of sizes, styles, and finishes. Pay attention not only to the fittings you like but the fixtures that complement them, and you'll be ready to dive right into selecting your own.

Fantastic fittings complete this picture-perfect bathroom.

The simple chrome towel bar and low-voltage light fixture suit the style and tone of the fittings.

Hand-held showerheads are convenient for users of all heights and abilities.

A two-handled, deck-mounted faucet and spout are positioned so they can be reached from outside or inside the tub.

Chrome, single-handle faucets are extremely popular because they're easy to use and easy to maintain. These long spouts extend well into the deep basins.

Sleek chrome fittings gleam in this contemporary setting. Each piece was chosen to suit the fixture it serves and to contribute to the overall picture. The two-handled tub fixture complements the single-handle sink faucets without being an identical match.

This bathroom clearly has been designed in accordance with universal design principals. A hand-held showerhead, easy-to-use faucet handles, clear spaces beneath the sinks, accessible storage, and a curbless shower welcome users of all abilities.

Sink Faucets

Like the right tie with a sharp suit or the perfect accessories with a stunning dress, a faucet enhances the appearance of a sink. The size, shape, style, and finish of each should complement the other.

The two factors that most affect faucet style are the number of handles and the shape and length of the spout. Traditional-style faucets have two handles while more contemporary-looking faucets often have one. Transitional styles work in many settings.

Once you've chosen a style, examine the construction and finish of the faucets you're considering. Generally, a well-made faucet will feel solid in your hands. The most durable faucets have solid-brass construction, corrosion-resistant finishes, and ceramic disc valves.

Mounted on a mirrored wall, these fittings seem to float above the spun glass bowl of a sink. Wall-mounted faucets are used in combination with sinks that don't have holes, such as vessel and under-mount sinks. Separate wall-mount valves and drains complete their installation.

Lever handles are easy to use, especially for people with limited hand strength. The arching design of this wide-spread faucet makes it delightfully attractive as well.

The tall, curved neck of this crescent faucet adds a bit of flair to the subtle elegance of this bathroom. Crescent, or gooseneck, faucets are best paired with deep basins that contain the fall of the water without excessive splashing.

*Idea*Wise

In extremely rustic or extremely contemporary settings, the water supply system can supply the fittings as well. Half-inch copper pipe, gate valves, and support brackets, typically used for rough plumbing, can be configured to deliver water right to a bathroom sink.

You can design a configuration to suit the space and sink, but here's the basic idea: Extend the hot and cold supply pipes to an opening at the center of the sink. In a convenient spot on each side, install a gate valve to control the flow of water.

Note: This high-concept idea may not be practical in homes that include children or adults with limited hand strength.

Brass fittings traditionally have been considered attractive but high maintenance because unprotected brass oxidizes when exposed to air. The protective lacquer and epoxy coatings developed to solve the problem were only partially successful because few of them stood up well to daily cleaning, especially abrasives.

New technology has been developed to give brass a finish that's as durable and easy to care for as chrome. Ask your designer, contractor, or retailer to make sure the fittings you're considering have the most durable finish possible.

Here, wide-spread brass sink and tub faucets glow against a neutral background.

Wide-spread faucets have two handles separate from the spout. Their size balances well with larger sinks and the space between pieces makes them easy to clean.

Powder-coated epoxy finishes are long lasting, easy to clean, and available in a variety of colors. Here, a white faucet virtually becomes part of a clean-lined pedestal sink.

Tub Faucets & Showerheads

Tub faucets and showerheads have contributions to make to the style of a bathroom, but their selection is fairly well determined by the selection of the sink faucets. However, there's still much to consider: placement, accessories, and—above all—safety.

Most building codes have requirements regarding scald protection on tub and shower fittings, and for good reason. Every day, in the United States alone, 300 young children are treated for burns resulting from hot water.

The reasons are not mysterious. Most manufacturers ship water heaters set at 140 to 150° F, and despite frequent warnings, many homeowners don't turn them down to the 120° F recommended by the National Safety Council. It takes only five seconds for a child to receive third-degree burns from water at 140°; two seconds at 150°.

The message here? Set your water heater at 120° F; replace any old valves with pressure-balancing valves that protect users from drastic temperature changes if someone flushes a toilet or runs water elsewhere in the house; if your household includes young children or elderly people, add safety-stop devices to your tub and shower faucets to limit how hot they can be set. And, of course, never leave young children unattended in a bathtub or shower.

Looking something like a genie's lamp, this deck-mounted faucet pours forth the soothing magic of warm water into a deep tub. When choosing a deck-mounted faucet, make sure its reach is adequate and its size proportional to the setting.

The graceful curves of these crescent spouts soften the angular lines of the counter and bath deck. The matching accessories are nice finishing touches for the room.

Fittings should be mounted on the side of tubs meant for two. That way, both ends of the tub offer plenty of room to lie back and relax.

Handsprays are wonderful conveniences for tubs. They're handy for washing a child's hair (or your own), as well as for rinsing the tub itself.

*Design*Wise

Trudy McCollum ASID, CKD, CBD

Kitchen and Bath Ideas
North Little Rock, AR

- There are a number of exciting new faucet finishes on the market today that will bring a sense of elegance and sophistication to your bathroom, including weathered copper, pewter, and black, French, or oil-rubbed bronze.

- Coordinate your cabinet pulls and knobs, towel bars and light fixtures with faucet finishes to bring an updated and unified look to your bathroom. And don't overlook the small items like toilet levers and the exposed stops, supply pipes, and P-traps of pedestal sinks. The details make the difference!

- Create a "mini spa" experience easily and inexpensively by swapping out your standard showerhead for a massage or rainspout showerhead. These fittings are now available with all the hardware you need to connect to the existing, standard plumbing.

- All retrofit tub and shower faucets must contain an anti-scald device, such as a pressure-balance valve, to protect bathers from being scalded by hot water or blasted with cold water when another fixture or appliance is in use.

Tub and shower combinations share water lines. A diverter valve directs water to either the tub spout or the showerhead. This space-saving combination is especially popular in children's and family baths.

This shower has something for everyone: a tall fixed head and an adjustable, hand-held head. Unlike many similar combinations, these heads are controlled independently and so could be run at the same time.

This is more than a shower, it's a watery world of its own.
Often called body spas, units like this include a showerhead as well as high-volume jets aimed for your head, neck, and trunk. In many such systems, the water is collected in the basin and recirculated, but they still require high-capacity water heaters, supply lines and drains.

CHAPTER 5

Lighting and Ventilation

Too often, bathroom lighting is merely an afterthought, purchased with whatever is left over in the budget after the surfaces, fixtures, and fittings are in place.

Big mistake. Huge. Good lighting makes bathrooms look better, but what may be more important is that good lighting makes us look better. For most of us, whatever time we spend reflecting on our reflections is spent in the bathroom. Shouldn't we cast the most flattering, color-correct light possible onto ourselves and our grooming routines?

Good bathroom lighting is more than mere vanity, though. Lighting actually can be a safety issue as well. Everyone—young and old—is less likely to fall or otherwise injure themselves in a well-lit room, especially if the light is set to reveal thresholds, steps, and areas that might be wet or slippery.

Like beauty, adequate lighting levels are in the eye of the beholder. Literally: The lenses of our eyes thicken and yellow as we age, so that by the age of 55, our eyes require twice as much light as they did at 20. Make an effort to create a lighting design that works for every member of the family today and well into the future.

Ventilation, another health and safety issue, is fundamental to bathrooms and should be designed into the plan from the very beginning of a project. Operable windows and mechanical ventilation improve the air we breathe and protect the structure itself from excess moisture.

Good bathroom lighting plans illuminate and enhance the features of the room as well as the features of the people who use the room. No one light source can accomplish such a feat—it takes layers of light produced by carefully planned and placed fixtures.

Natural and artificial light play off one another beautifully.

Skylights provide natural light from above. Some skylights, controlled by remote, also provide ventilation.

Vanity lighting is all about lighting the face, not the room. The best vanity lights are hung at eye-level on the side of the mirror.

These blinds can be closed for privacy, but windows provide both light and ventilation when desired. Whenever possible, at least 10 percent of a bathroom's light should be natural light.

Lampshades soften glare and cast more flattering light than bare bulbs or even globes.

Mirrors reflect and multiply light.

The skylight, windows, mirrors, and fixtures of this tropical themed bathroom team up to produce an effective, attractive lighting scheme.

Aim the beams at the outside edge of the tub to create pleasant, nonglare light for bathing.

Overhead fixtures provide the main source of light in the room.

(above) Recessed lights are not ideal as the main light source in a bathroom, but as supplemental sources, they positively shine. Here, recessed lights provide task lighting for specific areas such as the tub and toilet. To reduce glare and shadows, angle the bulbs to bounce off walls and ceilings.

Accent lighting draws attention to interesting architectural and structural features. Here, rope lighting behind cove molding highlights the molding and curved ceiling.

*Design*Wise

Jeff Livingston, LS
& Deborah Foucher Stuke, CLC
Luce Design Group
Manchester, NH

- A single source of light cannot perform all your lighting needs. Layer ambient, task, decorative, and accent light to create a properly illuminated room.

- Lighting should surround the face at the mirror. Fixtures placed 30 to 36" apart on the vertical plane provide even illumination and minimize shadows. Mounting heights vary depending on the fixture style and ceiling heights, but normally are centered at about 66" off the finished floor. For added interest, mount fixtures through the mirror. Avoid downlighting over the mirror as the only source lighting the face.

- Skin tones look best in warm light. Use incandescent sources or fluorescent sources with a color temperature of 3500K or less.

- Use dimming controls to provide variable light levels. Many dimmers have a "soft start" feature, which slowly raises the light level over a period of seconds to allow eyes to adjust to the light. A slow fade to "on" is nice for nighttime bathroom visits!

- Choose decorative fixtures with translucent lenses. Avoid clear glass, which produces glare, and colored glass, which will change the color of light reflecting on your face.

- Proper ventilation ensures healthy indoor air quality. The fan you select should be rated for the size of your room. To calculate the proper CFM (cubic feet per minute), multiply the square footage by 1.1 if the ceiling height is 8 feet. For ceilings over 8 feet, multiply the ceiling height by .1375, then multiply the square feet to determine the required CFM. Select a fan with at least this rating.

- Few things are more annoying in a bathroom than a noisy vent fan. Consider the noise (measured in sones) generated by the unit. One sone or less is recommended. Features such as timers, occupancy sensors, and humidity sensors are available for added comfort and convenience.

Vertical fluorescent fixtures

eliminate shadows when fitted with color-correct, full-spectrum bulbs. Here, the center of each fixture is positioned at eye level in order to cast flattering light across the face of a person using the sink.

The vanity fixtures should be spaced to illuminate both sides of the face equally, typically three to four feet apart.

Light fixtures throw dramatic shadows

through the clear glass of this countertop. To reduce shadows in the mirrors, each is illuminated from three directions: above, to the left, and to the right.

Mirror, mirror on the wall: What's the most flattering light of all?

Amber globes cast warm light akin to candlelight onto this powder-room mirror. The incandescent light above the mirror balances the color and reduces shadows.

Unique lighting fixtures like this are appealing in a powder room, but colored globes are not always ideal in a master or main family bathroom. In those bathrooms, frosted or clear textured glass provides better light for daily grooming routines.

Coordinating the light fixtures with the other fixtures in the room creates a heightened sense of style. The elliptical stainless steel sink, curved chrome faucet fittings, and arched arms of the light fixture go well together without exactly matching. Shopping for coordinated pieces makes a room more interesting and reflects more of your own personal taste than selecting pieces from a matching suite.

Strip lights above mirrors are extremely popular because they're inexpensive and low maintenance. They do not, however, always offer the most flattering light. If you choose strip lighting, reduce the glare by using frosted rather than clear bulbs.

*Idea*Wise

Read any magazine article or book on stress reduction these days, and you're bound to find that the list of prescribed cures includes long, relaxing soaks in a hot bath. If your idea of relaxing in the tub includes reading that magazine or book, you're going to need some light. Still, the glare of overhead lights may not be what you have in mind.

Install a small sconce or hard-wired library light on the side wall of the tub enclosure, on the end opposite the spout. Place the switch outside the tub enclosure, well out of reach so you won't be tempted to switch on the light while seated in the tub. Remember: Electricity and water DO NOT mix.

Shades cast more flattering light than bare bulbs. Frosted glass softens glare and shadows.

Full-spectrum light bulbs let you see in the mirror what others will see in the daylight.

Heat dissipates from the sockets of bulbs that face down, so bulbs tend to last longer.

Lamps must be placed far from sinks and other water sources and should be plugged into GFCI-protected receptacles.

(above) Lighting a dressing table mirror can be quite a challenge. In a large area such as this, sconces would be too far apart to provide adequate light, but strip fixtures above mirrors can produce glare and unflattering shadows. These homeowners solved the puzzle by using frosted globes on lights that face down rather than out, and by adding countertop lamps.

Dimmers are a good idea in every bathroom, but especially in a situation like this. Here, the fixtures can be dimmed and the lamps turned on for a softer, more relaxing atmosphere.

Whenever possible, natural light sources should contribute 10 percent of a room's ambient, or general, light. Get creative with glass block, traditional, or tubular skylights, and funky window combinations.

Operable windows topped by stationary transoms sparkle above a spacious soaking tub. These windows provide ventilation as well as light, since they can be opened to let moisture out and fresh air in.

It's a bit of a stretch, but these handles can be reached over the tub and bathers can easily reach them while seated in the tub. When choosing windows, consider their style of operation as well as their design style.

Let the sun shine in.

Bathroom windows present a challenge when it comes to window treatments. Some options are extremely expensive and others just aren't suited to a moist environment. Still, most of us are reluctant to leave bathroom windows completely uncovered, especially in neighborhoods where the houses are close together.

To provide privacy simply and inexpensively, buy an acid-etching kit at a craft store and etch the glass in a modesty zone on each window. If you're creative and imaginative you can do designs; if not, just etch a broad band or the whole window. Read and follow the manufacturer's directions carefully—these products can be caustic.

Tubular skylights deliver abundant natural light, a wonderful commodity in a bathroom that doesn't have other windows. The bathroom shown here includes a beautiful bank of windows in addition to the skylight, but many bathrooms don't include such riches.

Tubular skylights are reasonably priced and energy-efficient. Since they don't require any complicated framing, they're also easy to install. Some manufacturers use flexible plastic tubing that can be snaked around attic obstructions; others use solid plastic reflecting tubes that require more clearance. Evaluate your attic and roof as well as a range of these products before making a choice.

(right) The ideal lighting scheme combines natural and artificial light sources at a number of levels. Here, large windows provide natural light, a sconce provides light at eye level, and a fixture above the mirror provides task lighting. Shutters filter the natural light; frosted globes on the fixtures reduce glare as well.

An exhaust system provides mechanical ventilation for the room. In a heavily-used bathroom that has no windows or stationary windows only, it's wise to use a high-capacity ventilation system. The vent system should be capable of exchanging the air eight times per hour.

Large windows admit abundant light in this bathing alcove. The window combination was selected and set to frame the view, effectively bring the countryside into the room. Here, where privacy isn't an issue, window coverings are unnecessary.

CHAPTER 6

Accessories

Bathroom accessories are not strictly necessary in and of themselves: They're objects that add beauty, convenience, efficiency or effectiveness to the room. From a robe hook beside the tub to a lighted magnifying mirror next to the sink, accessories make daily routines just a little easier, more comfortable, or more enjoyable.

The key to accessorizing is balance: The pieces you choose should make the most of the space without overwhelming it. They should also complement the style and finish of fixtures and fittings in the room.

As you look through the photos in this chapter, think about your bathroom, the family members who use it, and the daily routines. Imagine what would make life more pleasant as you start and end each day. Perhaps you'd like a reading light near the tub or toilet, a stack of baskets to hold hand towels and wash cloths, or even a towel warmer to take the chill off winter mornings. All those things and more are available.

Mirrors, hooks, baskets, storage pieces—they all contribute to the ambience as well as the efficiency of this eclectic bathroom.

Placing the center of the mirror at eye level makes it easy to use.

Well-placed hooks make it easy to keep bathrooms neat and organized.

Bathroom accessories simplify daily living.

Live flowers and green plants freshen and sweeten the air and the atmosphere.

Small lamps add a cozy glow to bathrooms.

Throw rugs absorb water and provide a soft, warm spot for bare feet. They should be slip-resistant and easy to launder.

Baskets keep magazines and other reading material collected and close at hand.

Mirrors multiply the available light, especially when they're placed opposite or adjacent to windows. Here, a generous mirror is positioned to bounce light off the angles of the ceiling and walls, a very clever strategy.

A textured glass panel in the door protects privacy without totally blocking light. It's a lovely touch in this well-lit room, but would be especially welcome in a bathroom without windows.

A small shelf behind the sink is especially useful when counterspace is limited.

Wall-mounted cup holders and soap dishes save precious space in small bathrooms.

Tilted mirrors allow seated or short users to easily see themselves.

The towel racks match the style and finish of the faucet, light fixtures, and cup brackets.

Brackets hold drinking cups near the sink.

Mirrored medicine cabinets provide handy, easy-to-reach storage space. One caveat regarding this or any other medicine cabinet: Cleaning supplies and medications should always be stored in cool, dry, lockable space.

Adjustable, lighted magnifying mirrors bring delicate grooming tasks into focus. The tiniest details—stray eyebrows, nose hairs, even that bit of spinach between your teeth—are clearly visible in devices like this.

A sturdy bar beneath the counter makes it easy for seated users to pull themselves into position. The bar can hold hand towels and washcloths.

A bathroom should have at least 24" of towel bar for each person who regularly uses it. At least one bar or hook should be positioned within 12" of a shower or tub.

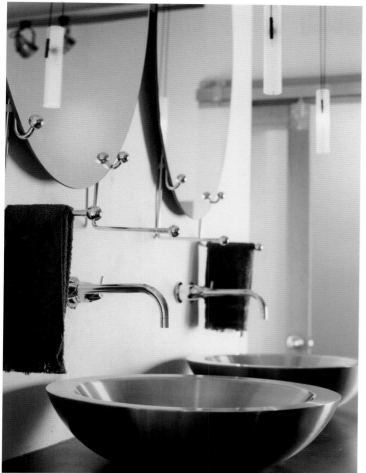

Extensions of the mirror brackets, these towel racks hold towels right where they're needed.

Warm towels may be the ultimate luxury when you step from a shower or tub. Some models must be hard wired and some require plumbing connections, but free-standing, plug-in models are widely available as well.

Whatever style you choose, make sure it's UL listed and properly installed. Free-standing models should be plugged into GFCI-protected outlets.

This plumbing riser extends to support a track for the shower curtain, a very clever arrangement for this free-standing tub. The braces for the riser are secured to studs behind the wood paneling with sturdy anchors.

It might not seem like weight is an issue—after all, it's only a shower curtain. Except it's not just the shower curtain you're supporting. A set-up like this should be prepared to support the weight of someone who uses it to steady himself or grabs it while falling.

Shower curtains can be far more than a ubiquitous plastic panel from the discount store. Many ready-made curtains are made from easy-care fabrics that dry quickly and hold their color well. Backed by a sturdy liner, such curtains can be graciously draped over an attractive curtain rod or standard shower rod.

Free-standing tubs often lack places to keep bathing supplies. Here, a chrome basket neatly solves that problem. The accent table and the chair also provide spaces to keep supplies and comforts.

Recessed light fixtures highlight the tile shower and glass door.

The lines of the mirror frame echo the trim around the shower, integrating the two.

The wooden slats on the shower bench are a subtle but effective coordinating touch.

When counter space is limited, accessories can provide creative solutions. Here, the vanity counter and trough sink are long on style but a bit short on space. A wooden tray effectively divides the sink and provides a place to set toiletries and other grooming necessities.

Using wood to match the vanity makes it clear the tray is part of the design rather than an afterthought.

For those who can't wake up without talk radio or music, audio speakers in the shower are a fantastic choice. These are, of course, special components built to withstand exposure to moisture and heat.

In some circumstances it would be possible to retrofit speakers into a shower, but the best time by far to add them is during new construction or a major remodel. Upper-end designers report that most new bathrooms à la family rooms and home theaters are being wired for sound these days.

*Design*Wise

Lori Jo M. Krengel, CKD, CBD
Kitchens by Krengel, Inc.
St. Paul, MN

- Bathroom mirrors have come a long way in recent years, from anti-fog and magnifying features to TV and computer monitors built into or projected onto the surface.

- When planning for towel bars, don't just mount them in whatever space is available. Rather, consider the size and function of the towel, then install a towel bar large enough to allow towels to be hung to dry properly.

- Towel bars with warmers can act as space heaters in small bathrooms.

- Many homeowners are installing two toilet paper holders at each location for convenience.

ACCESSORIES

(left) Good design has a starting point, an anchor. The design of this powder room is based on the unique hand-painted vanity. The color and shape of the mirror, wall sconces—even the towel ring—take their cues from the curves and scrolls of the painted design. Notice that while the pieces don't precisely match, they clearly were chosen to complement one another.

*Idea*Wise

Reading in the tub isn't always as relaxing as one might hope, what with trying to keep the book out of the water and in a comfortable position. No problem. Keep your books and magazines high and dry with a custom-built bookstand.

Measure the width of your tub, then cut a piece of 3/4" teak about 10 inches wide and long enough to fit across the tub. Cut two 10 × 2" cleats of teak and secure one cleat near each end of the tray, using glue and 1¼" screws. Sand the tray, apply a coat of teak oil, and let the oil dry according to manufacturer's instructions. (You could also purchase a tray to fit across the tub, if you can find one the right size.)

Use silicone caulk to secure a clear acrylic cookbook stand to the tray, about an inch from the front.

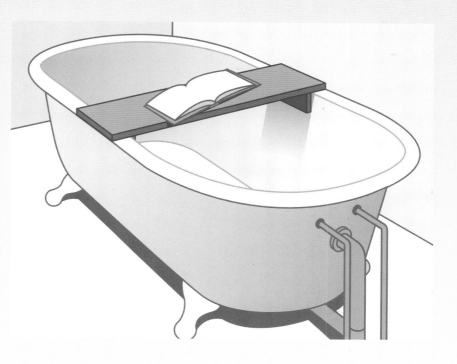

Resource Guide

A listing of resources for information, designs, and products found in *IdeaWise Bathrooms*.

Introduction

page 7:
Forma bathtub by:
Jason International
1-800-255-5766
www.jasoninterational.com/

page 8:
Bathroom fixtures and fittings by:
Kohler Co.
1-800-4-KOHLER
www.kohlerco.com

Walls, Floors and Ceilings

page 20 (top):
Concrete tiles by:
Buddy Rhodes Studio, Inc.
San Francisco, CA
877-706-5303
www.buddyrhodes.com

page 24 (both):
Vinyl flooring by:
Armstrong Flooring
Armstrong World Industries
717-397-0611
www.armstrong.com

page 29:
DeWitt Talmadge Beall
Dewitt Designer Kitchens
12417 Ventura Boulevard
Studio City, CA 91604
818-505-6901
www.dewittdesignerkitchens.com

page 30 (both):
Concrete tiles by:
Buddy Rhodes Studio, Inc.
San Francisco, CA
877-706-5303
www.buddyrhodes.com

Storage and Display

page 43:
Pat Currier
Currier Kitchens & Baths
135 Route 101A, Carriage Depot
Amherst, NH 03031
603-883-2407
www.currierkitchens-baths.com

page 47:
Bathroom fixtures and fittings by:
Kohler Co.
1-800-4-KOHLER
www.kohlerco.com

page 55:
Countertop and backsplash by:
DuPont Corian
1-800-4-CORIAN
www.corian.com

page 57 (bottom):
Glass tile by:
Crossville, Inc.
931-484-2110
www.crossvilleinc.com

page 58 (bottom):
Concrete countertop by:
Buddy Rhodes Studio, Inc.
San Francisco, CA
877-706-5303
www.buddyrhodes.com

Resource Guide

(continued)

Fixtures

page 65:
Glass tile by:
Crossville, Inc.
931-484-2110
www.crossvilleinc.com

page 67:
Countertop by:
DuPont Corian
1-800-4-CORIAN
www.corian.com

page 68 (left):
Tile by:
Crossville, Inc.
931-484-2110
www.crossvilleinc.com

page 68 (right):
Italian tile by:
Ceramic Tiles of Italy
212-980-1500
www.italytile.com

page 72-73 (both):
Bathroom fixtures and fittings by:
Kohler Co.
1-800-4-KOHLER
www.kohlerco.com

page 74:
Italian tile by:
Ceramic Tiles of Italy
212-980-1500
www.italytile.com

page 77:
Tile by:
Crossville, Inc.
931-484-2110
www.crossvilleinc.com

page 78 (bottom):
Concrete panels by:
Buddy Rhodes Studio, Inc.
San Francisco, CA
877-706-5303
www.buddyrhodes.com

page 79:
Italian tile by:
Ceramic Tiles of Italy
212-980-1500
www.italytile.com

pages 80-81:
Tile by:
Crossville, Inc.
931-484-2110
www.crossvilleinc.com

pages 84-85:
Bathroom fixtures and fittings by:
Kohler Co.
1-800-4-KOHLER
www.kohlerco.com

page 85:
Linda Burkhardt
Kitchens & Baths by Linda
771 Montauk Hwy., Suite 2
Montauk, NY 11954
631-668-6806
www.lindaburkhardt.com

page 86 (top):
Shower and countertop by:
DuPont Corian
1-800-4-CORIAN
www.corian.com

page 88:
Italian tile by:
Ceramic Tiles of Italy
212-980-1500
www.italytile.com

page 89 (bottom):
Bathroom fixtures and fittings by:
Kohler Co.
1-800-4-KOHLER
www.kohlerco.com

page 91 (bottom):
Bathroom fixtures and fittings by:
Kohler Co.
1-800-4-KOHLER
www.kohlerco.com

Fittings

page 103:
Bathroom fixtures and fittings by:
Kohler Co.
1-800-4-KOHLER
www.kohlerco.com

page 105:
Trudy McCollum, ASID, CKD, CBD
Kitchen and Bath Ideas
8800 Maumelle Blvd., Suite B
North Little Rock, AR 72113
501-812-0200
trudy@kitchenandbathideas.biz

Lighting and Ventilation

page 113:
Jeff Livingston, LS
Deborah Foucher Stuke, CLC
Luce Design Group, LLC
PO Box 132
Manchester, NH 03105
603-821-5853
www.lucedesigngroup.com

page 115:
concrete countertop by:
Buddy Rhodes Studio, Inc.
San Francisco, CA
877-706-5303
www.buddyrhodes.com

page 119:
vinyl casement and
transom window unit by:
JELD-WEN
1-800-JELD-WEN
www.jeld-wen.com

Accessories

page 120:
Suntunnel skylight by:
VELUX-America, Inc.
1-800-88-VELUX
www.velux-america.com

page 126 (bottom):
tilted mirror by:
Ginger
1-888-469-6511
www.gingerco.com

page 132:
concrete countertop by:
Buddy Rhodes Studio, Inc.

San Francisco, CA
877-706-5303
www.buddyrhodes.com

page 133:
Lori Jo Krengel, CKD, CBD
Kitchens by Krengel
1688 Grand Avenue
St. Paul, MN 55105
651-698-0844
www.kitchensbykrengel.com

Photo Credits

Front cover and title page: © Brian Vanden Brink for Hutker Architects.

Back cover: (top left) Brand X Pictures; (top right) © getdecorating.com; (center) Kohler Co.; (bottom left) Photo courtesy of Armstrong World Industries/ Armstrong Flooring; (bottom right) Photo courtesy of Ceramic Tiles of Italy.

p. 2: Photo courtesy of Armstrong World Industries/ Armstrong Flooring.

p. 3: (left) © Getty Images, (right) photo courtesy of Crossville Inc.

p. 4: © David Livingston/ davidduncanlivingston.com.

p. 7: Photo courtesy of Jason International.

p. 8: Photo courtesy of Kohler Co.

p. 9: © David Livingston/ davidduncanlivingston.com.

p. 10: © Todd Caverly photographer/ Brian Vanden Brink Photos for George Snead Jr. Interior Design.

p. 12: © Brand X Pictures.

pp. 14-15: © getdecorating.com.

p. 16: © Brian Vanden Brink for Dominic Mercadante, Architect.

p. 17: (top) © getdecorating.com; (bottom) © Brian Vanden Brink for for John Morris, Architect.

p. 18: Photo courtesy of Crossville Inc.

p. 19: © David Livingston/ davidduncanlivingston.com.

p. 20: (top) Photo courtesy of Buddy Rhodes Studio, Inc.; (bottom) photo courtesy of Crossville Inc.

p. 21: © getdecorating.com.

p. 22: (both) © Brian Vanden Brink, for (top) Sam Van Dam, Architect; (bottom) Chris Glass, Architect.

p. 23: © Brand X Pictures.

p. 24: (both) Photos courtesy of Armstrong World Industries/ Armstrong Flooring.

p. 26: (top) Photo courtesy of Crossville Inc.; (bottom) © David Livingston/ davidduncanlivingston.com.

p. 27: © getdecorating.com.

p. 28: © Brian Vanden Brink for John Colamarino, Architect.

p. 29: © getdecorating.com.

p. 30: (both) Photo courtesy of Buddy Rhodes Studio, Inc.

p. 31: © Brian Vanden Brink for Elliott Elliot Norelius Architecture.

p. 32: (both) © Brian Vanden Brink, for (bottom) Centerbrook Architects.

p. 33: (both) © Brian Vanden Brink.

p. 34: © Brian Vanden Brink for Mike Homer, Architect.

p. 35: © Brian Vanden Brink.

p. 36: © getdecorating.com.

pp. 38-39: (both) © getdecorating.com.

pp. 40-41: © getdecorating.com.

p. 42: © Brian Vanden Brink for Axel Berg, Builder.

p. 43: © Brian Vanden Brink for South Mountain Co. Builders.

p. 44: © Brian Vanden Brink.

p. 45: (both) © Brian Vanden Brink, for (top) for Seegin, Elam, & Bray, Architects; (bottom) Sally Westin, Architect.

p. 47: Photo courtesy of Kohler Co.

p. 48: © Brian Vanden Brink for Sally Westin, Architect.

p. 49: © Brian Vanden Brink for Sally Westin, Architect.

p. 50: (both) © Brian Vanden Brink, for (top) Morningstar Marble & Granite; (bottom) Elliot Elliot Norelius Architecture.

p. 51: © Brian Vanden Brink.

p. 52: © Brian Vanden Brink.

p. 53: © Brian Vanden Brink.

p. 54: © Brian Vanden Brink for Drysdale Assoc., Interior Design.

p. 55: Photo courtesy of Dupont TM Corian®.

p. 56: © getdecorating.com

p. 57: (top) © Brian Vanden Brink for Tom Hampson Builder; (bottom) photo courtesy of Crossville Inc.

p. 58: (top) © David Livingston/ davidduncanlivingston.com; (bottom) photo courtesy of Buddy Rhodes Studio, Inc.

p. 59: © David Livingston/ davidduncanlivingston.com; (bottom) © Brian Vanden Brink.

p. 60: © getdecorating.com.

pp. 62-63: © Brian Vanden Brink for Dominic Mercadante, Architect.

p. 64: © Todd Caverly for G.M. Wild Builders.

p. 65: Photo Courtesy of Crossville Inc.

p. 66: © Brian Vanden Brink for Elliot Elliot Norelius Architecture.

p. 67: Photo courtesy of Dupont TM Corian®.

p. 68: (left) Photo courtesy of Crossville Inc.; (right) photo courtesy of Ceramic Tiles of Italy.

p. 69: © Brian Vanden Brink for Morningstar Marble & Granite.

p. 70: (left) © Brian Vanden Brink for Peter Bohlin, Architect; (right) © Getty Images.

p. 71: (both) © Brian Vanden Brink, for (top) Green Company Architects; (bottom) John Morris, Architect.

pp. 72-73: (both) Photo courtesy of Kohler Co.

Index

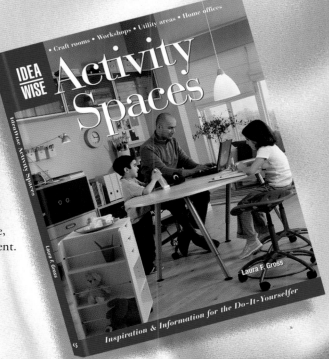

Also from

CREATIVE PUBLISHING INTERNATIONAL

Complete Guide to Bathrooms
Complete Guide to Building Decks
Complete Guide to Ceramic & Stone Tile
Complete Guide to Creative Landscapes
Complete Guide to Easy Woodworking Projects
Complete Guide to Finishing Touches
  for Yards & Gardens
Complete Guide to Flooring
Complete Guide to Home Carpentry
Complete Guide to Home Masonry
Complete Guide to Home Plumbing
Complete Guide to Home Storage
Complete Guide to Home Wiring
Complete Guide to Kitchens
Complete Guide to Outdoor Wood Projects
Complete Guide to Painting & Decorating
Complete Guide to Roofing & Siding
Complete Guide to Windows & Doors
Complete Photo Guide to Home Repair
Complete Photo Guide to Home Improvement
Complete Photo Guide to Outdoor Home Repair

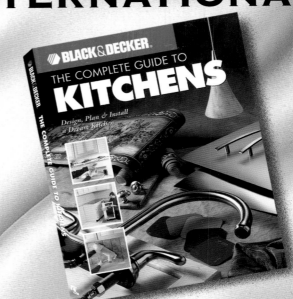

ISBN 1-58923-138-4

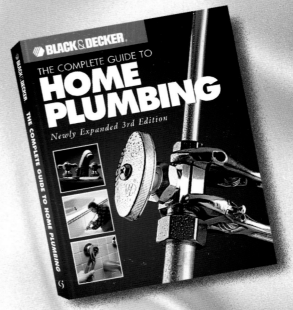

ISBN 0-86573-428-3

CREATIVE PUBLISHING INTERNATIONAL

18705 LAKE DRIVE EAST
CHANHASSEN, MN 55317

WWW.CREATIVEPUB.COM